# THE KEMETIC CODE™

A Revolutionary System of Energetic
and Spiritual Healing for the Afrikan Diaspora

By:
AKILI WORTHY

© 2025 Akili Worthy Worldwide LLC. All Rights Reserved.

No part of this book may be copied, reproduced, distributed, or transmitted in any form or by any means, including photocopying, recording, or other electronic or mechanical methods, without the prior written permission of the publisher, except in the case of brief quotations used in book reviews and other non-commercial uses permitted by copyright law.

Published by Akili Worthy Worldwide LLC

This book is for informational and educational purposes only. The author and publisher are not responsible for any specific health or medical outcomes based on the application of the information contained in this book. Readers should consult with a qualified professional before beginning any new wellness, energy healing, or health-related practices.

All rights reserved.

For more information, visit: spiritualblackgirl.com

# Table of Contents

Introduction: Reclaiming Our Ancestral Healing ............ 5

Chapter 1: Understanding the Foundation of *The Kemetic Code™* ................................................................ 9

Chapter 2: The Theft & Appropriation of Our Sacred Wisdom ............................................................................ 21

Chapter 3: The 9 Sacred Energy Centers ...................... 31

Chapter 4: Applying Energy Healing to Daily Life .......... 67

Chapter 5: Using the Kemetic Code™ & Collective Healing ............................................................ 75

Chapter 6: Maintaining Energy Mastery & Long-Term Spiritual Evolution ................................... 89

Chapter 7: Embodying the Kemetic Code™ & Elevating Collective Consciousness ............................. 97

Chapter 8: Trusting Your Path & Embracing Future Evolution ............................................................ 105

CHAPTER 9: THE POWER OF ENERGY HEALING –
REAL STORIES OF TRANSFORMATION ........................................... 113

EPILOGUE: BECOMING THE CODE ................................................ 125

APPENDIX ....................................................................................... 129

WORKS CITED ................................................................................ 135

ABOUT THE AUTHOR ..................................................................... 137

INVITATION TO PRACTITIONER TRAINING ................................... 139

ACKNOWLEDGMENTS .................................................................... 141

# Introduction:
## Reclaiming Our Ancestral Healing

---

For centuries, the healing wisdom of our African ancestors has been suppressed, distorted, and rebranded under other names. Energy healing, muscle testing, and vibrational medicine—all of which have deep African roots—have been stripped from our cultural identity, leaving many of us disconnected from our own birthright. *The Kemetic Code*™ exists to change that.

I created *The Kemetic Code*™ because I saw a gap—a missing piece in how Black people connect to energy healing and emotional release work. While techniques like Reiki, acupuncture, and the chakra system are widely accepted, their African origins and predecessors are rarely acknowledged. I knew there had to be a way to uncover what was ours, in a system that honored our history, our people, and our ancestral wisdom.

At the same time, I saw a need for a structured yet accessible healing method—one that did not require years of study or an external guru to facilitate. *The Kemetic Code*™ empowers individuals to heal themselves using the same universal laws and energetic principles that our ancestors understood thousands of years ago. This is not a new system—it is a restoration of what was lost.

## THE RISING DEMAND FOR ENERGY HEALING

The world is waking up to what our ancestors always knew: energy governs all things. The growing interest in energy healing is proof that people are searching for deeper, more holistic ways to heal. Consider the following:

- A 2022 survey found that over 40% of Americans have used complementary and alternative medicine (CAM), including energy healing techniques like Reiki and acupuncture.

- The global energy healing market is projected to grow significantly, reflecting increasing acceptance of non-traditional healing methods.

- Studies show that Reiki and other biofield therapies can reduce stress, improve mood, and enhance well-being in clinical settings.

- Research from the National Institutes of Health (NIH) suggests that biofield therapies influence the autonomic nervous system, reducing stress-related conditions.

- Studies on Applied Kinesiology (muscle testing) have shown it can be effective in detecting subconscious stressors and emotional blocks.

While these findings are promising, what's missing from the conversation is the acknowledgment of African contributions to energy healing. *The Kemetic Code*™ is about restoring our place in this global awakening—ensuring that Black people are not only included in the conversation but leading it.

## How This Book Will Transform You

This book is designed to do more than educate—it is a guide to your own transformation. By the time you finish, you will:

- Understand how energy flows within your body and how to align it for optimal health and clarity.

- Learn to identify and release emotional Knots—the energetic blockages preventing you from stepping into your full power.

- Discover how to use muscle testing to connect with your subconscious mind, unlocking deeper healing.

- Connect to the African spiritual wisdom that has been hidden from you for too long.

*The Kemetic Code*™ is about empowerment. It puts the tools of healing back in your hands—where they have always belonged.

It is time to claim what was stolen.
It is time to remember who you are.

# A Message to the Reader

You didn't find this book by accident.
You are here to remember.
*The Kemetic Code*™ is not a healing method.
It is a return to Post-Interruption Possibility—
a future unbound by trauma, illusion, or limitation.
It is a sacred framework for unlearning the lie
and remembering who you were before the interruption.
We don't treat symptoms.
We restore sovereignty.
We don't cope with systems.
We step outside them.
We don't fix broken people.
We awaken gods and goddesses who were never meant to forget.
You are not here to survive a lie.
You are here to remember a truth so ancient, so infinite,
it could never be colonized.
You are the rebirth.
You are the blueprint.
You are the continuation of greatness that never truly stopped—
only paused, only hidden, only waiting.
**Welcome to** *The Kemetic Code*™.

# Chapter 1:
## Understanding the Foundation of *The Kemetic Code*™

---◆---

*"The body heals with play, the mind heals with laughter, and the spirit heals with joy."*

– African Proverb

For thousands of years, the ancient Kemetic civilization understood the intricate relationship between energy, healing, and spiritual balance. Their healers, priests, and priestesses were not just medical practitioners but also energetic alchemists who worked with *Sekhem*—the life force energy—to restore health and harmony. Unlike modern healing systems that often separate the physical from the spiritual, the Kemetians saw no such division. To heal the body, one must also heal the energy.

Over time, much of this sacred knowledge was lost due to colonization, cultural suppression, and historical revisionism. As a result, many of the energetic healing practices that originated in Africa have been misattributed to other spiritual traditions. But the wisdom of our ancestors remains encoded within us, waiting to be remembered and activated.

*The Kemetic Code*™ was created as a bridge—reconnecting us to the energy healing systems of our ancestors while making them accessible for modern use. This book serves as both a guide and a reclamation of an ancient practice that has always belonged to us. Whether you are seeking personal healing, looking to deepen your spiritual practice, or wanting to help others, *The Kemetic Code*™ provides a structured, intuitive, and powerful approach to working with energy.

Through this journey, you will learn how to identify and clear energetic blockages, realign with your divine essence, and activate your full potential. The goal is to restore harmony within yourself and within the collective consciousness of the African diaspora. Healing is not only possible; it is our birthright.

## THE PRINCIPLE OF MA'AT: LIVING IN DIVINE ALIGNMENT

One of the most fundamental aspects of Kemetic wisdom is *Ma'at*, the cosmic principle of balance, truth, order, and harmony. *Ma'at* is more than just a concept; it is a way of life that ensures alignment between the spiritual, mental, emotional, and physical realms. It is the force that maintains balance in the universe, and when we align with it, we restore balance within ourselves.

Ma'at

## MA'AT IN PRACTICE: EMBODYING DIVINE ALIGNMENT

In Kemet, *Ma'at* was personified as a goddess, depicted with an ostrich feather on her head—a symbol of lightness, truth, and divine justice. But *Ma'at* was also a living principle, embedded in daily actions, laws, and spiritual practices. Every aspect of Kemetic society, from governance to personal ethics, was guided by *Ma'at*.

## PRACTICAL WAYS TO EMBODY MA'AT IN DAILY LIFE

- **Speak and act with integrity** — Commit to truth and righteousness in your words and actions.

- **Seek balance** — Avoid extremes in emotions, thoughts, and behaviors. Recognize when you are out of alignment and correct course.

- **Honor relationships** — Treat others with fairness, kindness, and respect, understanding that harmony is key to collective well-being.

- **Live in alignment with nature** — Recognize that the universe operates in cycles and rhythms. Honor your body, mind, and spirit by living in tune with these natural laws.

- **Practice gratitude and reciprocity** — Give freely, knowing that what you put out into the world will return to you. A life in *Ma'at* is a life in divine flow.

## MA'AT AND THE 9 SACRED ENERGY CENTERS

In *The Kemetic Code*™, we recognize that energetic blockages create disharmony, leading to emotional, physical, and spiritual distress. Following *Ma'at* provides the framework for restoring balance within our 9 Sacred Energy Centers, ensuring that *Sekhem* energy flows freely.

Each energy center governs specific aspects of our being. When we live in alignment with *Ma'at*, we maintain harmony in these centers, promoting:

- Mental clarity and wisdom (*Sekhem* energy at the crown)

- Emotional stability and compassion (Heart center)

- Creative and personal power (Solar energy center)
- Groundedness and security (Root energy center)

By practicing *Ma'at*, we naturally clear knots (energetic blockages) and restore balance within these centers, leading to a life of greater peace, clarity, and alignment.

## THE ORIGINS OF KEMETIC ENERGY HEALING

The ancient Kemetic civilization (modern-day Egypt) possessed a profound understanding of energy, healing, and the connection between the spiritual and physical worlds. This knowledge was embedded in their daily lives, temple practices, and medical treatments. Healers, priests, and priestesses utilized *Sekhem*, the life force energy, to restore balance and well-being. The Kemetic worldview recognized that all **dis-ease** stemmed from energetic imbalances, and restoring *Ma'at*—universal order—was key to healing.

The temples of Kemet, particularly those dedicated to Imhotep and other great healers, served as centers of medical and spiritual learning. Texts such as the *Ebers Papyrus* document advanced medical knowledge, demonstrating that Kemetic healers understood the intricate connections between body, mind, and spirit long before modern science acknowledged such links.

In these sacred spaces, the use of *Sekhem* energy was integral to both spiritual and physical well-being. Healers engaged in hands-on energy transfers—a predecessor to modern Reiki—using sacred symbols and chants to channel the life force. These practitioners also incorporated herbal medicine, vibrational sound healing (using chanting and *sistrums*, or sacred rattles), and sacred geometry in their healing rituals.

These methods did not simply treat symptoms; they addressed the spiritual causes of illness, ensuring holistic healing.

## TEMPLE HEALING PRACTICES AND THE ROLE OF ENERGY

The temples of Kemet were centers of advanced healing, education, and energetic mastery. The *Per Ankh*, or "House of Life," functioned as both a school and a sanctuary where sacred knowledge of medicine, astronomy, and metaphysics was preserved. Here, initiates studied the connection between energy, the elements, and the human body.

Priests and priestesses trained for years to master the use of *Sekhem* energy, learning how to assess imbalances in the body through observation, touch, and divination techniques. Healing ceremonies were performed in alignment with celestial movements, acknowledging the cosmic forces that influenced human health. They utilized:

- **Sacred sound frequencies** — Chanting specific tones to activate healing frequencies and clear energetic blockages.

- **Crystal and mineral therapy** — Placing specific stones, such as lapis lazuli and carnelian, on the body to amplify *Sekhem* energy.

- **Water purification rituals** — Using sacred pools to cleanse the physical and spiritual bodies before energy work.

- **Herbal remedies infused with intention** — Preparing medicinal tonics that carried vibrational healing properties.

Healing was seen as a divine process that involved aligning the individual's life force with *Ma'at*, restoring balance within the mind, body, and soul.

## THE CONNECTION BETWEEN KEMETIC AND OTHER AFRICAN HEALING TRADITIONS

Although much of the written record from Kemet has been fragmented or lost due to historical invasions and colonial disruption, many African spiritual and healing traditions still carry the echoes of Kemetic wisdom. These traditions are not isolated but deeply interconnected, evolving from a shared foundation of African metaphysical understanding.

- **Yoruba (West Africa)** — The concept of *Ase'*, like *Sekhem*, represents the divine life force that animates all existence. Yoruba healers call upon *Ase'* to empower rituals, infuse herbal medicine with energy, and restore spiritual balance.

- **Zulu Sangomas (Southern Africa)** — These spiritual healers use vibrational chanting, rhythmic drumming, and invocations to align individuals with ancestral energy and clear emotional blockages—mirroring Kemetic sound healing.

- **Dagara (Burkina Faso)** — The Dagara practice energetic purification through elemental rituals involving fire, water, air, and earth—echoing Kemetic purification rites.

- **Bantu-speaking groups (Central and Southern Africa)** — Their traditions incorporate dreamwork, divination, and ancestral healing, all rooted in the same spiritual science that once thrived in the temples of Kemet.

These shared practices affirm that *The Kemetic Code*™ is not just about remembering a distant past—it's about reconnecting with an unbroken lineage of African spiritual healing. The knowledge already exists in many forms. Our work is to recognize, reclaim, and re-integrate it for modern empowerment and wholeness.

## Moving Forward with Ma'at

*The Kemetic Code*™ is more than a healing system—it is a way of inserting *Ma'at* into our lives. It is about remembering that balance, truth, and alignment are not just ideals, but practices that shape our reality. As you move through this book, let *Ma'at* be your guide, leading you back to your highest self and divine power.

Understanding and applying *Ma'at* is the foundation of Kemetic energy healing, the 9 Sacred Energy Centers, and all the work we will explore moving forward. With this knowledge, you are now ready to begin the journey of energetic mastery and spiritual restoration. I've included one Law of *Ma'at* at the end of each chapter, and a complete list of all 42 Laws in the Appendix. Our people understood that powerful living starts from the inside and radiates outward.

## Real-World Stories of Transformation

As we go deeper into the work, I want to provide you with some real-world examples of those who are using *The Kemetic Code*™ today. You may find some similarities between their stories and your own. It's possible their journeys will serve as a source of inspiration—at least, they did for me.

## Akili's Journey: Remembering the Path

In 2016, I began my formal journey into energy healing by studying hypnotherapy. I was fascinated—finally learning about the subconscious mind and how it could be accessed for deep healing without medication felt like unlocking a hidden truth. After receiving my certification, I became hungry for more. I immersed myself in Reiki, astrology, numerology, and oracle cards. I didn't just study—I became a reader myself, and even worked in metaphysical bookstores, including one that was Black-owned and steeped in rich cultural energy.

It was in those spaces that I experienced sound healing, runes, and healing circles for the first time. I connected with other Black intuitives, acupuncturists, sound healers, and spiritual guides. Still, I noticed that beyond these rare spaces, the broader metaphysical world lacked color. When I attended psychic fairs or spiritual expos, I often felt like the very practices rooted in our heritage were being distorted or commercialized. Something in me knew: this wasn't just about learning healing—it was about reclaiming it.

Eventually, I stepped away from the metaphysical world, feeling like I didn't belong. But my gifts kept calling. No matter how much I tried to "return to the real world," Spirit wouldn't let me forget who I was. The vision for *The Kemetic Code*™ began to crystallize—not only as a return to our ancestral wisdom but as a pathway home for Black healers, seekers, and visionaries who needed language, structure, and spiritual permission to remember what was ours all along.

## REAL-LIFE TRANSFORMATIONS WITH *THE KEMETIC CODE*™

### AUTUMN'S STORY: HEALING ANXIETY AT 17

Autumn had always been an overachiever, excelling in academics and extracurriculars. However, beneath her success lay a deep struggle with anxiety. From a young age, she experienced panic attacks that made it difficult to concentrate in school. Crowded spaces, exams, and even social interactions triggered overwhelming fear, leaving her feeling powerless. Her parents sought help through therapy and medication, but nothing seemed to bring lasting relief.

Feeling desperate for change, Autumn and her mother explored alternative healing methods, leading them to The Kemetic Code™. Through muscle testing, she discovered that her anxiety was linked to an ancestral Knot connected to fear and uncertainty passed down through her maternal lineage. Through guided Sekhem energy clearing, she was able to release the trapped fear from her energy field.

Within weeks, Autumn noticed a shift. Her panic attacks became less frequent, and she started feeling more confident in high-stress situations. Over time, she developed a sense of calm she had never known before. Now, she actively integrates The Kemetic Code™ into her daily life, using breathwork and energy alignment techniques to maintain emotional balance. Today, she no longer sees anxiety as a controlling force in her life but as something she has learned to transmute into self-empowerment.

## Genesis' Story: Overcoming Self-Doubt at 32

Genesis had always been creative, full of big dreams and ambition. However, she struggled deeply with self-doubt, preventing her from acting on her goals. She found herself constantly second-guessing her ideas, hesitating to speak up, and feeling unworthy of success. These feelings of inadequacy stemmed from childhood experiences where she was often told she wasn't "good enough."

As Genesis entered adulthood, this pattern continued to hold her back. She avoided leadership roles at work, turned down opportunities out of fear of failure, and felt stuck in a cycle of procrastination. After hearing about The Kemetic Code™ from a friend, she decided to explore it, hoping for a breakthrough.

Through muscle testing, she discovered that her self-doubt was tied to a Knot in her solar energy center, blocking her ability to recognize her worth. This Knot was connected to generations of women in her family who had internalized messages of inadequacy. After working with me and engaging in a series of Sekhem energy clearings, she felt an internal shift.

For the first time in years, Genesis found herself stepping into her power. She started confidently expressing her ideas at work, taking risks, and launching a business she had been dreaming of for years. The voices of self-doubt that once paralyzed her grew quieter, and she began trusting herself. Today, she uses The Kemetic Code™ not just for herself but to help other women break free from self-limiting beliefs and claim their full potential.

## Jason's Story: Releasing Chronic Stress at 49

For over two decades, Jason had battled recurring stress headaches. As a corporate executive, his demanding job left him feeling overwhelmed and constantly on edge. He rarely took breaks, worked long hours, and carried the weight of high-pressure decisions. No amount of pain relievers, massages, or lifestyle changes provided lasting relief. His stress had become a constant companion, affecting his relationships, sleep, and overall well-being.

Frustrated with conventional treatments, Jason sought out energy healing and found The Kemetic Code™. Through muscle testing, he uncovered that his headaches were tied to an ancestral Knot connected to suppressed anger and unprocessed grief. He had inherited a pattern of emotional suppression from the men in his family, who had been taught to "stay strong" and not express their emotions.

Through Sekhem energy clearing, Jason was able to release these deep-seated emotions. The first session brought an immediate sense of lightness, and within weeks, his headaches significantly decreased. Over time, he began sleeping better, feeling more present in his relationships, and managing stress with greater ease. Jason now integrates The Kemetic Code™ into his daily routine, ensuring that stress no longer rules his life. He describes the experience as nothing short of life changing.

## EXPANDING THE PATH TO ENERGETIC MASTERY

These are just a few stories that showcase how *The Kemetic Code*™ is a powerful tool for personal and collective healing—offering those in the African Diaspora a means to reconnect with their ancestral wisdom and reclaim their birthright to wholeness.

Understanding the foundational principles of energy healing is just the beginning. To fully harness this power, we must deepen our knowledge of the 9 Sacred Energy Centers—the gateways through which *Sekhem* energy flows.

These centers, much like the energetic systems found in other ancient traditions, hold the key to physical vitality, emotional balance, and spiritual enlightenment. By learning to identify and clear blockages in these centers, we can fully activate our divine potential and step into alignment with *Ma'at*.

In the next chapter, we will delve into the 9 Sacred Energy Centers, their significance, and how they can be utilized for healing and transformation.

# Chapter 2:
## The Theft & Appropriation of Our Sacred Wisdom

*"Until the lion learns to write, every story will glorify the hunter."*
— African Proverb

The knowledge embedded within The Kemetic Code™ is not new—our ancestors understood energy, healing, and sacred alignment long before these concepts were studied by the outside world. Yet, much of this sacred wisdom was deliberately stolen, erased, or repackaged under different names. The erasure of Kemetic spirituality was not accidental—it was a calculated effort to disconnect Black people from their divine heritage and the power that comes with it.

This chapter explores how Kemetic wisdom was extracted, distorted, and rebranded by external cultures, but more importantly, it provides actionable steps for learning and protecting this knowledge. Reclaiming this wisdom is not just about the past—it is a revolutionary act of restoration, self-liberation, and spiritual sovereignty.

## The Erasure & Distortion of Kemetic Spirituality

The destruction of Kemetic knowledge was intentional and methodical. Temples were defaced, spiritual texts were burned, and oral traditions were disrupted. Those who carried the sacred teachings—priests, healers, and scholars—were often persecuted or forced into hiding. What was once an expansive spiritual system, known throughout the ancient world, was deliberately dismantled to weaken the people it empowered.

Kemetic spirituality and healing were systematically eradicated through colonization, religious conquest, and cultural suppression. Over centuries, powerful empires sought not just to dominate African land and resources but also to control its people by severing them from their spiritual foundations.

**The Greeks & Romans:** These civilizations studied in Kemet, extracting its wisdom and rebranding it as their own. Figures like Pythagoras, Plato, and Hippocrates learned directly from African scholars, but their societies erased the acknowledgment of their sources.

Kemet's advanced knowledge in mathematics, medicine, and philosophy was appropriated and incorporated into Greek and Roman traditions, often without credit to the African masters who originally developed these disciplines. The very foundation of Western intellectualism was built upon Kemetic teachings—yet history has largely omitted Africa's central role in shaping these fields.

**The Catholic Church & European Colonization:** With the rise of Christianity and later European imperialism, Kemetic teachings were actively suppressed. Temples were destroyed, texts were burned, and African spiritual leaders were labeled as heretics or pagans.

This systematic erasure was not just about religion—it was a tool for control. By stripping Africans of their indigenous knowledge systems, colonizers ensured spiritual and intellectual dependency on European institutions. Many of the foundational Christian doctrines and iconography—including the concept of the Trinity and the Madonna and Child—were directly influenced by Kemetic spiritual traditions, yet their origins were deliberately obscured.

**The Whitewashing of Kemet:** European historians worked hard to disconnect Kemet from its African roots, portraying its people as non-Black and distorting historical records. This deliberate act of historical revisionism reinforced the false idea that African civilizations contributed little to world knowledge.

From 19th-century Egyptology to modern media portrayals, the image of Kemet has been systematically altered to fit Eurocentric narratives. Even today, museum exhibits, academic texts, and films often depict the ancient Kemetians with European features—erasing the undeniable African presence in one of the world's greatest civilizations.

This whitewashing was not accidental—it was a calculated effort to diminish Africa's historical and cultural legacy on a global scale.

The goal of these efforts was clear: if Black people forgot who they were, they would be easier to control. This erasure was not only about history—it was about spiritual disconnection. When a people no longer remember their supreme inheritance, they become vulnerable to systems of oppression.

I often wonder what our world would look like today if Kemetic spiritual systems had been allowed to flourish—if Black people had never been disconnected from this wisdom. If we were never interrupted.

# How Kemetic Teachings Were Stolen & Rebranded

Despite these attempts to erase Kemetic wisdom, remnants of its teachings survived—passed down through oral traditions, hidden symbols, and practices preserved in secret. Though much of its original structure was lost, echoes of its spiritual and healing systems can still be found in other traditions—many of which refuse to acknowledge their true origins.

Many spiritual concepts that originated in Kemet were later repackaged under Western and Eastern traditions, with little to no acknowledgment of their African origins.

## Kemetic Influence on Western Esoteric Traditions

**Hermeticism & Freemasonry:** The teachings of Hermes Trismegistus, a Greek name for the Kemetic deity Tehuti (Thoth), became the foundation for Western occultism, secret societies, and esoteric philosophy.

The *Emerald Tablet* of Tehuti (Thoth), which became foundational in later Hermetic philosophy, originated from Kemetic wisdom, outlining the idea of "As above, so below."

**Alchemy & Sacred Geometry:** The principles of alchemy and sacred geometry—which later became central to European mystical traditions—originated in Kemet. The ancient Kemetic priests and scholars understood that the universe operates on mathematical precision, and that transformation—both spiritual and physical—is governed by divine laws.

## ALCHEMY: THE SCIENCE OF SPIRITUAL & MATERIAL TRANSFORMATION

- In Kemet, alchemy was not just about turning lead into gold—it was about spiritual purification and energetic mastery.

- The term *alchemy* itself comes from the Arabic *Al-Kimiya*, which refers to the Black Land (Kemet), acknowledging its African roots.

- The Kemetic concept of transformation involved aligning with Ma'at (divine balance) and refining the self to reach a higher vibrational state, mirroring the later Western pursuit of enlightenment.

## SACRED GEOMETRY: THE MATHEMATICAL BLUEPRINT OF THE UNIVERSE

- The pyramids, temples, and hieroglyphic inscriptions of Kemet were designed with precise geometric ratios, reflecting divine harmony.

- The Ankh, the Flower of Life, and the Djed Pillar were not just spiritual symbols—they were mathematical and energetic codes representing life force, creation, and stability.

- The Golden Ratio (Phi) and Fibonacci sequence, which later influenced Greek and Renaissance art and architecture, were already encoded in Kemetic temples thousands of years before they appeared in European thought.

- The movement of celestial bodies was also mapped using sacred geometry, influencing later Western astrology and astronomy.

## REVISED APPROACH TO EASTERN SPIRITUAL TRADITIONS

**The Chakra System:** While often associated with Indian traditions, the understanding of energy centers in the body can be traced back to Kemetic teachings on the 9 Sacred Energy Centers. As African people traveled and interacted with Asia, this wisdom was carried with them, influencing the energetic systems that later became codified in Indian and other Eastern traditions.

## AKILI'S REFLECTION

I remember my first Reiki session. The practitioner was skilled in so many ways. As she moved over each chakra, it was like an energy healing session and a reading. She was especially drawn to the energy center right below my navel. She said that area was cold. And she was right.

Over the years, I've had several womb-related challenges—from infertility that was healed to the loss of pregnancy late in my second trimester. There were definitely layers of trauma I hadn't fully addressed. I couldn't believe she knew it—but the energy was clearly blocked.

She spent extra time sending energy to that area to aid in the healing, and I was blown away by what she was able to pick up. That experience stayed with me and reminded me how real energy is—how much the body holds, and how essential it is that we have healing spaces that truly understand the sacredness of this work, especially for Black women.

**Meditation & Breathwork:** Long before yogic traditions formalized breath control, Kemetic priests practiced Sekhem breathwork as a method for activating life force energy and maintaining spiritual alignment. This ancient practice shares commonalities with later pranayama techniques found in Indian spiritual systems.

**Vibrational Healing:** Many energy-based healing systems—such as Reiki—share striking similarities with Kemetic healing practices. Rather than being separate discoveries, these traditions may have stemmed from a common African origin that evolved uniquely in different parts of the world.

## Protecting Our Spiritual Legacy

When I learned about Kemet, my whole worldview changed. The way I felt about who we are and who we were was forever altered. Racism and white supremacy have always been ridiculous notions and practices to me. However, once I learned about the extensive theft our people experienced, I just looked at us as pure genius—incredible people who had been terrorized in the worst way. And we will take our rightful place.

Understanding *The Kemetic Code*™ is about healing and restoring our spiritual sovereignty. By reconnecting with these teachings, we actively break the cycle of historical erasure and reawaken the divine knowledge encoded in our DNA.

## Actionable Steps to Reawaken & Protect This Wisdom

Instead of just recognizing the theft, we must take action to reclaim what was lost. Here's how you can actively participate in restoring and protecting Kemetic wisdom:

- **Support Black Spiritual Leaders & Scholars** – Seek out and uplift Black teachers who are reviving Kemetic wisdom through books, courses, and online communities.

- **Research African Spiritual Traditions** – Read primary sources, study the Pyramid Texts and *The Book of Coming Forth by Day*, and explore indigenous African spiritual systems.

- **Practice Kemetic Spirituality Daily** – Incorporate meditation, breathwork, Sekhem energy healing, and Ma'at-centered living into your routine.

- **Educate & Share Knowledge** – Teach your children, family, and community about Kemetic wisdom so that future generations do not have to rediscover it.

- **Build & Engage in Black-Owned Platforms** – Create spaces where this knowledge is preserved, discussed, and celebrated without distortion.

- **Honor Your Ancestors** – Set up an ancestor altar, engage in ancestral veneration, and seek guidance from those who came before you.

- **Challenge Historical Misinformation** – Speak out when you see Kemetic wisdom being appropriated or misrepresented.

## Why This Reclamation Matters

By bringing this knowledge back into our awareness, we break the cycle of erasure and step back into our role as the architects of our own reality. Here are some ways this may manifest:

- **Healing Generational Wounds:** Reconnecting with Kemetic wisdom repairs the spiritual damage caused by centuries of oppression.

- **Returning to Our True Power:** When Black people reclaim their Ma'atic knowledge, they restore the ability to create, heal, and manifest with intention.

- **Ensuring Future Generations Have Access to This Wisdom:** If we do not protect and preserve our spiritual legacy, it will continue to be stolen and distorted.

*The Kemetic Code*™ is a movement to restore what was taken and ensure that our descendants never have to search for their sacred inheritance again.

This book is a step toward that restoration. **You** are a part of this reclamation.

# Chapter 3:
## The 9 Sacred Energy Centers

*"A person who has health has hope,
and a person who has hope has everything."*

— African Proverb

### Unlocking Divine Alignment

Since the earliest days of Kemetic civilization, the understanding of energy and balance has been deeply woven into spiritual and healing practices. The concept that energy flows through the body—and that blockages can lead to physical, emotional, and spiritual imbalances—is an ancient truth. The Kemetians, through their advanced wisdom, identified **9 Sacred Energy Centers** that serve as the key to maintaining harmony within oneself and with the Most High.

These energy centers are more than theoretical concepts; they are **living forces within us** that influence our emotions, health, and ability to manifest our highest potential. When in alignment, they allow **Sekhem**, the supreme life force, to flow freely—promoting well-being and spiritual clarity. However, when blocked, they can manifest as anxiety, self-doubt, physical ailments, and disconnection from one's purpose.

Unlike the more commonly known chakra system, which consists of seven energy centers, the Kemetic system aligns with the principle of **Ma'at**—order, balance, truth, and harmony. The number nine holds deep spiritual significance, representing **completion, wisdom, and transformation**. Each of the 9 Sacred Energy Centers corresponds to a specific aspect of human existence—from our sense of security and creative expression to our ability to receive divine insight.

Throughout history, the knowledge of these energy centers was intentionally suppressed, buried beneath layers of colonization and cultural erasure. However, this wisdom has not been lost—it is still within us, **encoded in our very being**, waiting to be remembered and activated. By working with these energy centers, we reconnect with the ancient Kemetic tradition of energy healing and bring it back home.

In the following sections, we will explore each of the 9 Sacred Energy Centers in depth. We will examine their purpose, the signs of balance and imbalance, and the practical techniques—such as **Sekhem energy work, affirmations, movement, and breathwork**—that can be used to restore and maintain alignment.

Additionally, muscle testing—specifically the **Finger Rings Test** and **Alternating Finger Test**—plays a key role in identifying blockages in these centers. While a brief mention of these tests will be made here, a more detailed explanation of how to perform them will be provided in Chapter 5.

Through this knowledge, we gain the power to heal ourselves, embody divine order, and fully step into our highest potential.

## Understanding Knots: The Barriers to Energy Flow

In *The Kemetic Code*™, we refer to **Knots** as energetic blockages that obstruct the natural movement of Sekhem energy through the 9 Sacred Energy Centers. Just as a tangled knot in a water hose prevents an even and easy flow of water, these blockages disrupt balance, hinder spiritual growth, and manifest as emotional, mental, or physical distress.

## How Knots Form

Knots can develop in several ways:

- **Emotional Trauma** – Painful experiences, unresolved grief, or suppressed emotions create dense energy in the body, preventing the free flow of Sekhem.

- **Limiting Beliefs** – Negative thought patterns, fear-based conditioning, and self-doubt constrict energy flow and prevent expansion.

- **Ancestral Imprints** – Unresolved generational wounds or inherited traumas pass down as energetic Knots, influencing one's emotional and spiritual state.

- **Disconnection from Ma'at** – When one moves away from truth, harmony, and divine balance, energetic misalignment occurs, leading to stagnation.

- **Unprocessed Physical Stress** – Chronic fatigue, poor diet, lack of movement, and toxic environmental influences create Knots that weaken the body's energy field.

## My First Experience Clearing Knots

As I was developing *The Kemetic Code*™, I remember when I first started clearing the Energy Knots. In my very first session, I was able to unravel six Knots: **Fear, Insecurity, Shame, Emotional Numbness, Low Self-Esteem**, and **Resentment**. These energies were present in my field, and my body was ready to let them go.

During the releases, I found myself taking deep, intentional breaths—it just felt like the natural thing to do. While I didn't consciously feel the release of every single emotion, I could definitely sense that some were heavier than others.

What surprised me the most happened a few hours later: **I felt giddy**. And let me be clear—I'm a serious person, up to serious things. Giddy is not my usual state. But there I was, smiling for no reason—light, buoyant, free. I hadn't felt that kind of joy in a long time—not without a reason to justify it. It felt like every worry had evaporated. And in its place was **trust. Peace. A deep sense that everything was unfolding exactly as it should.**

That's when I knew—this wasn't just a practice. This was a path. A sacred one. And I believe every one of us deserves to feel that kind of release. That kind of lightness. That kind of freedom.

## Effects of Knots in the Sacred Energy Centers

Each of the 9 Sacred Energy Centers governs a specific aspect of human experience. When a Knot forms in one of these centers, it leads to imbalances that manifest in predictable ways:

- **First Energy Center (Root):** Feelings of fear, instability, financial struggles, chronic stress, or immune system issues.

- **Second Energy Center (Sacral):** Creative blocks, difficulty in relationships, sexual dysfunction, or suppressed emotions.

- **Third Energy Center (Solar Plexus):** Low self-esteem, lack of motivation, digestive issues, or chronic self-doubt.

- **Fourth Energy Center (Heart):** Emotional detachment, inability to trust, grief, resentment, or heart-related physical ailments.

- **Fifth Energy Center (Throat):** Difficulty expressing oneself, fear of speaking one's truth, sore throats, or thyroid issues.

- **Sixth Energy Center (Third Eye):** Confusion, poor intuition, difficulty making decisions, or frequent headaches.

- **Seventh Energy Center (Crown):** Spiritual disconnection, cynicism, lack of purpose, or chronic mental exhaustion.

- **Eighth Energy Center (Ancestral Gateway):** Feeling lost in one's identity, unresolved family trauma, or difficulty receiving ancestral guidance.

- **Ninth Energy Center (Divine Connection):** Feeling separate from the universe, existential crises, or an inability to manifest one's highest purpose.

## CLEARING KNOTS AND RESTORING BALANCE

Thankfully, Knots are not permanent—they can be **cleared, healed, and released** through intentional energy work, self-awareness, and Kemetic healing practices. Some of the most effective ways to dissolve Knots and realign with Ma'at include:

- **Sekhem Energy Healing** – Directing Sekhem life force into blocked areas to restore energetic flow.

- **Sacred Sound Healing** – Using vibrational frequencies, chanting, and sistrum sounds to shift stagnant energy.

- **Movement & Breathwork** – Engaging in Kemetic Yoga postures and deep breathing to clear energetic congestion.

- **Affirmations & Intentions** – Reprogramming limiting beliefs and replacing them with empowering, Ma'at-aligned thoughts.

- **Ancestral Healing** – Engaging in ritual and connection with ancestors to clear inherited energetic Knots.

By understanding and working with Knots, we take an **active role in our healing journey**, ensuring that Sekhem energy flows freely and harmoniously through our being. This is how we embody Ma'at—not just as an idea, but as a **lived experience of balance, truth, and divine alignment**.

With this foundational knowledge, we are now ready to explore each of the **9 Sacred Energy Centers** in depth. The following sections will guide you through their significance, signs of balance and imbalance, and practical methods for maintaining alignment.

**Let us begin with The First Sacred Energy Center: The Seat of Grounded Stability.**

## THE FIRST SACRED ENERGY CENTER: THE SEAT OF GROUNDED STABILITY

The First Sacred Energy Center represents the foundation of existence. In Kemet, this energy center was understood as the anchor that connects the human spirit to the physical world—much like the **Djed Pillar**, an ancient symbol of stability and endurance. The Djed was associated with **Ausar (Osiris)**, the divine archetype of resurrection and balance, signifying the power of rootedness and inner strength.

This energy center is located at the perineum, between the genitals and the anus, but it also activates the base of the spine, where the **Djed Energy Pathway** begins. It governs feelings of safety, security, and stability. It is the center that ties us to the physical world, ensuring that we feel grounded and supported in our daily lives.

In ancient Kemet, initiates of spiritual schools were taught that without a strong foundation, higher wisdom could not be fully integrated. They would undergo rituals designed to strengthen their connection to the earth, affirming their place in the cosmic order of **Ma'at**.

## Signs of Balance

When the First Sacred Energy Center is in balance, a person feels:

- Grounded and present in their body
- Confident in their ability to meet their basic needs
- A sense of safety and trust in the universe
- Strong physical health and vitality

## Signs of Imbalance

When this energy center is blocked or weak, it can manifest as:

- Chronic fear, anxiety, or insecurity
- Financial instability or struggles with survival needs
- Feeling disconnected from the body or ungrounded
- Physical symptoms such as lower back pain, fatigue, or issues with the feet and legs

- Helplessness, detachment, survival anxiety, unworthiness, doubt

## Root Causes of Imbalance

Imbalances often stem from deep-rooted experiences that create feelings of instability or fear:

- **Fear** – A heightened sense of danger or insecurity
    - *Causes:* Childhood instability, ancestral trauma, unpredictable environments
- **Insecurity** – Persistent lack of safety or support
    - *Causes:* Emotional or financial insecurity in childhood, feeling unloved
- **Instability** – Difficulty maintaining life balance
    - *Causes:* Frequent moves, changing caregivers, lack of routine
- **Helplessness** – Belief that one lacks control over life
    - *Causes:* Repeated failure, oppression, learned powerlessness
- **Detachment** – Disconnection from emotions or others
    - *Causes:* Trauma, emotional suppression, neglect
- **Survival Anxiety** – Constant fear of scarcity
    - *Causes:* Poverty, abandonment, generational scarcity mindset
- **Unworthiness** – Belief of being undeserving of love or stability
    - *Causes:* Criticism, comparison, systemic oppression

- **Disconnection** – Feeling separated from self, community, or ancestry
  - *Causes:* Cultural loss, assimilation, loneliness
- **Doubt** – Lack of trust in self or the world
  - *Causes:* Betrayal, disappointment, dependence on external approval

## Ways to Restore Balance

- **Grounding practices:** Walk barefoot on earth (Earthing), or practice Kemetic Yoga to strengthen the legs
- **Affirmations:** "I am safe. I am supported. I am rooted in divine stability."
- **Sekhem energy work:** Place hands at the lower spine, visualize golden Sekhem energy flowing in
- **Nourish with grounding foods:** Beets, sweet potatoes, purple carrots
- **Sacred rituals:** Meditate on the Djed Pillar, practice earth-honoring ceremonies

By strengthening this energy center, we create a stable foundation for all other aspects of our being, ensuring that we move through life with confidence and alignment with Ma'at.

In the next section, we will explore the Second Sacred Energy Center, which governs creativity, emotional flow, and the power of sacred relationships.

## The Second Sacred Energy Center: The Source of Creativity and Sacred Relationship

The Second Sacred Energy Center governs **creativity, emotional expression, and sacred relationships**. In Kemet, this center was linked to **the waters of Nun**—primordial cosmic waters from which all creation emerged. As life sprang from these divine waters, this center represents our **creative flow, emotional depth, and capacity for intimacy**.

Located in the lower abdomen, near the womb or reproductive organs, this center reflects the fluid nature of existence. It was associated with **Het-Heru (Hathor)**—goddess of beauty, joy, love, and artistic expression. Temples dedicated to her included sacred spaces for music, dance, and rituals, showing that **pleasure and creative expression were divine forces.**

### Signs of Balance

When this center is balanced, a person experiences:

- Emotional freedom and self-expression
- Creative inspiration in life and relationships
- A strong sense of sensuality and joy
- Deep, fulfilling emotional and physical connections

### Signs of Imbalance

- Creative blocks or lack of inspiration
- Emotional suppression or hypersensitivity
- Fear of intimacy or relationship challenges

- Physical issues: reproductive problems, urinary tract conditions, lower back pain

## Root Causes of Imbalance

- **Guilt** – Emotional weight preventing joy
    - *Causes:* Shame-based upbringing, religious restrictions
- **Repression** – Suppressed desire or creativity
    - *Causes:* Fear of judgment, trauma, cultural taboos
- **Creative Blockages** – Lack of inspiration or motivation
    - *Causes:* Perfectionism, fear of failure, over-criticism
- **Emotional Numbness** – Emotional disconnection
    - *Causes:* Grief, prolonged stress, trauma shutdown
- **Shame** – Feeling unworthy of joy or pleasure
    - *Causes:* Body image issues, sexual repression
- **Lack of Pleasure** – Disconnection from joy
    - *Causes:* Burnout, guilt, overworking
- **Suppressed Desires** – Holding back emotional or sensual urges
    - *Causes:* Fear of rejection, religious guilt
- **Fear of Intimacy** – Avoiding closeness
    - *Causes:* Betrayal, abandonment, early neglect
- **Avoidance** – Distracting from emotions

- *Causes:* Fear of feeling, unresolved pain

## Ways to Restore Balance

- **Creative expression:** Paint, dance, write, sing

- **Affirmations:** "I am a divine creator. My emotions flow freely. I embrace pleasure and joy."

- **Water connection:** Ritual baths, sit near natural waters

- **Movement:** Kemetic Yoga poses that open hips and pelvis

- **Sacred support:** Meditate on Het-Heru; decorate space with symbols of water and creativity

# The Third Sacred Energy Center: The Seat of Personal Power and Divine Will

The Third Sacred Energy Center governs **personal power, self-discipline, and divine will**. In Kemet, it was linked to **Ra (Re)**—the sun deity symbolizing vitality, sovereignty, and the sacred force of creation.

Located at the **solar plexus**, this center serves as our inner sun. It fuels confidence, transforms thought into action, and empowers us to lead with truth. Initiates were taught to cultivate this energy to build resilience, uphold Ma'at, and manifest purpose.

## Signs of Balance

- Strong self-confidence and purpose

- Clear decision-making and personal direction

- Healthy boundaries and inner strength

- Motivation and spiritual alignment

## Signs of Imbalance

- Self-doubt or powerlessness
- Indecision or avoidance
- Over-controlling or arrogant behavior
- Digestive issues, chronic fatigue, stomach discomfort

## Root Causes of Imbalance

- **Self-Doubt** – Uncertainty in one's power
  - *Causes:* Harsh criticism, past failures, perfectionism
- **Lack of Motivation** – Feeling uninspired or aimless
  - *Causes:* Burnout, fear of failure, conformity pressure
- **Fear of Failure** – Risk avoidance
  - *Causes:* Punishment for mistakes, rejection
- **Low Self-Esteem** – Feeling "not enough"
  - *Causes:* Neglect, societal messages
- **Feeling Powerless** – Disempowerment
  - *Causes:* Oppression, trauma, controlling environments
- **Indecisiveness** – Inability to commit
  - *Causes:* Past mistakes, lack of self-trust

- **External Validation Seeking** – Needing approval
    - *Causes:* Childhood invalidation, societal conditioning
- **Over-Control** – Domination to avoid vulnerability
    - *Causes:* Trauma, ego defenses
- **Victim Mentality** – Blame and helplessness
    - *Causes:* Disempowering experiences, repeated trauma

## Ways to Restore Balance

- **Sun meditation:** Soak in sunlight, visualize golden solar energy
- **Affirmations:** "I stand in my power. I align with divine purpose. I trust myself completely."
- **Core activation:** Breathwork and Kemetic Yoga for the core
- **Sekhem energy healing:** Place hands over solar plexus; envision radiant sun
- **Solar-charged foods:** Lemons, bananas, turmeric, ginger
- **Sacred symbols:** Work with symbols of Ra or carry solar imagery

# The Fourth Sacred Energy Center: The Gateway to Love and Divine Connection

The Fourth Sacred Energy Center governs **love, compassion, and divine unity**. In Kemet, it was connected to **Ma'at**, the principle of truth and balance that upheld cosmic and personal harmony.

Located at the **heart center**, it bridges the physical and spiritual. Love was seen not just as an emotion but as a **universal force**—capable of healing, transforming, and elevating consciousness.

## Signs of Balance

- Emotional peace and inner harmony
- Unconditional love for self and others
- Deep connection to the divine
- Healthy, open relationships
- Intuition guided by love

## Signs of Imbalance

- Fear of connection or intimacy
- Resentment, grief, emotional shutdown
- Emotional detachment or clinginess
- Heart, lung, or circulatory issues

## Root Causes of Imbalance

- **Resentment** – Holding past pain
    - *Causes:* Betrayal, feeling unappreciated
- **Grief** – Emotional pain from loss
    - *Causes:* Death, heartbreak, ancestral sorrow

- **Emotional Numbness** – Lack of feeling
  - *Causes:* Trauma, grief, emotional overload
- **Loneliness** – Isolation
  - *Causes:* Fear of vulnerability, past abandonment
- **Unworthiness** – Feeling undeserving of love
  - *Causes:* Neglect, rejection, shame
- **Heartbreak** – Lingering sadness
  - *Causes:* Romantic betrayal, family conflict
- **Isolation** – Emotional withdrawal
  - *Causes:* Shame, depression, exhaustion
- **Lack of Empathy** – Disconnection from others' emotions
  - *Causes:* Burnout, emotional suppression
- **Inability to Trust** – Reluctance to open up
  - *Causes:* Betrayal, disappointment, abandonment

## Ways to Restore Balance

- **Heart meditation:** Visualize pink or green light radiating love
- **Affirmations:** "I am love. My heart is open. I trust divine connection."
- **Kindness rituals:** Acts of service, gratitude, forgiveness
- **Sekhem energy healing:** Place hands over chest, breathe into heart space

- **Nourishment:** Leafy greens, avocado, hibiscus or rose teas
- **Sacred tools:** Feather of Ma'at, rose quartz, malachite

## THE FIFTH SACRED ENERGY CENTER: THE SEAT OF DIVINE EXPRESSION AND TRUTH

The Fifth Sacred Energy Center governs **communication, self-expression, and the ability to speak divine truth**. In Kemet, this center was associated with **Tehuti (Thoth)**, the deity of wisdom, speech, and sacred knowledge. Tehuti was revered as the keeper of divine language, responsible for recording cosmic law and guiding human understanding through clear and truthful expression.

Located at the **throat**, this energy center bridges the heart and mind. It enables us to express our inner truth and aligns us with the power of the spoken word. The ancient Kemetians understood that words carried **vibrational frequencies capable of shaping reality**. Sacred chants, prayers, and hieroglyphic inscriptions were tools of spiritual transformation.

When this energy center is in balance, we speak with **clarity, confidence, and authenticity**. We listen deeply and express ourselves with power. When blocked, however, we may struggle with dishonesty, fear of speaking, or feeling unheard.

### SIGNS OF BALANCE

When this energy center is in balance, a person experiences:

- The ability to communicate clearly and effectively
- Confidence in expressing thoughts and emotions
- Alignment between thoughts, words, and actions

- The capacity to listen deeply and with empathy
- A strong connection to divine wisdom and intuitive messages

## Signs of Imbalance

When this energy center is blocked or excessive, it may manifest as:

- Fear of speaking or difficulty articulating thoughts
- Over-talking, gossiping, or dominating conversations
- Inability to listen or engage in meaningful dialogue
- Suppression of one's truth, feeling misunderstood or ignored
- Physical symptoms such as throat pain, voice loss, or thyroid imbalances

## Root Causes of Imbalance

Imbalances in this energy center often stem from fear of rejection, suppression of truth, and struggles with self-expression.

- **Fear of Speaking** – Hesitation when expressing thoughts or feelings
    - *Causes:* Childhood silencing, fear of judgment, past ridicule
- **Dishonesty** – Difficulty telling the truth
    - *Causes:* Fear of conflict, fear of consequences, learned manipulation
- **Holding Back** – Resisting full expression due to fear of judgment
    - *Causes:* Feeling ignored, invalidation, past trauma

- **Suppressed Expression** – Difficulty articulating emotions or needs
  - *Causes:* Cultural conditioning, fear of rejection, silence in upbringing
- **Social Anxiety** – Discomfort in social settings due to fear of speaking
  - *Causes:* Embarrassment, exclusion, low self-confidence
- **Avoidance of Confrontation** – Difficulty asserting oneself
  - *Causes:* Fear of arguments, trauma from verbal conflict
- **Over-Explaining** – Feeling the need to defend or justify oneself
  - *Causes:* Fear of being misunderstood, perfectionism
- **Feeling Unheard** – Frustration when one's voice is ignored
  - *Causes:* Childhood neglect, toxic relationships, marginalization

## Ways to Restore Balance

To strengthen and realign this energy center, one can:

- **Vocal expression:** Chanting, singing, or reciting affirmations aloud
- **Affirmations:** "I speak my truth with clarity and confidence. My voice carries divine wisdom."
- **Practice deep listening:** Cultivate awareness by hearing others without needing to respond immediately

- **Sekhem energy work:** Place hands over the throat and visualize a glowing blue light

- **Throat-supportive nourishment:** Herbal teas, honey, pears, and cooling foods like cucumber

- **Sacred symbols:** Meditate on Tehuti's symbol or write sacred words as spiritual practice

By restoring this center, we reclaim the **power of truth, clarity, and sacred speech**. Through our words, we co-create reality and contribute to the collective harmony of **Ma'at**.

## THE SIXTH SACRED ENERGY CENTER: THE GATEWAY TO INNER VISION AND HIGHER WISDOM

The Sixth Sacred Energy Center governs **intuition, inner vision, and spiritual perception**. In Kemet, it was associated with the **Udjat Eye (Eye of Heru)**—also called the Third Eye—symbolizing spiritual sight, clarity, and the ability to **see beyond illusion**.

Located at the **forehead**, just above the brow, this center holds the wisdom of **inner knowing**. The Kemetians understood that true wisdom came not just from external sources but through dreams, ancestral guidance, and cosmic awareness. Initiates in the mystery schools underwent sacred rites to awaken this vision and access higher truths.

When balanced, we experience **clear intuition, spiritual insight, and purpose**. When blocked, we may feel lost, confused, or unable to trust our inner voice.

## Signs of Balance

- Trust in intuition and inner knowing
- A clear sense of spiritual direction
- Vivid dreams and access to spiritual messages
- Insightful decision-making
- Connection to ancestral and cosmic wisdom

## Signs of Imbalance

- Confusion, indecision, or lack of direction
- Over-reliance on logic or others' opinions
- Disconnection from spiritual guidance
- Paranoia, fear-based thoughts, or overactive imagination
- Physical symptoms: headaches, vision problems, sinus pressure

## Root Causes of Imbalance

Imbalances stem from fear of seeing the truth, mental overstimulation, or disconnection from intuitive guidance.

- **Confusion** – Feeling lost or unable to decide
  - *Causes:* Overwhelm, excessive input, lack of trust in intuition

- **Disconnection from Intuition** – Doubting inner guidance
  - *Causes:* Social conditioning, past invalidation

- **Paranoia** – Irrational suspicion or fear
  - *Causes:* Trauma, prolonged stress, mental fatigue
- **Lack of Clarity** – Foggy perception or tunnel vision
  - *Causes:* Mental clutter, resistance to spiritual insight
- **Closed-Mindedness** – Rigid beliefs, fear of new ideas
  - *Causes:* Cultural programming, mistrust
- **Overthinking** – Excessive analysis, worry, or hesitation
  - *Causes:* Perfectionism, unresolved anxiety
- **Skepticism** – Disbelief in spiritual or unseen truths
  - *Causes:* Religious trauma, societal conditioning
- **Mental Fog** – Inability to focus or recall
  - *Causes:* Exhaustion, emotional overload, poor nutrition
- **Distrust of Self** – Questioning one's instincts or judgments
  - *Causes:* Childhood invalidation, manipulation, disempowerment

## Ways to Restore Balance

- **Meditate on the Udjat Eye:** Visualize the Eye of Heru opening within the forehead
- **Affirmations:** "I see clearly. My intuition guides me with wisdom and clarity."

- **Dreamwork and journaling:** Record dreams and spiritual insights regularly

- **Stillness practices:** Breathwork and quiet meditation to calm mental chatter

- **Sekhem energy healing:** Place hands on the third eye, visualize indigo light

- **Support with foods:** Blueberries, grapes, eggplants—foods that support the third eye

- **Sacred symbols and allies:** Meditate with the Udjat Eye or invoke Heru for clarity

By working with this energy center, we restore **clarity, insight, and divine vision**—reclaiming our intuitive gifts and seeing the truth behind the veil.

## THE SEVENTH SACRED ENERGY CENTER: THE BRIDGE TO DIVINE CONNECTION

The Seventh Sacred Energy Center is the gateway to divine consciousness, universal wisdom, and spiritual enlightenment. In Kemet, this center was associated with Amun-Ra—the hidden, all-encompassing force of creation.

Located at the crown of the head, it connects the personal self with cosmic intelligence. The Kemetians understood that true wisdom came from direct experience of the divine, not just knowledge. Temples were sacred places to activate this center and align one's mind with divine will.

When this energy center is balanced, we feel spiritually connected, at peace, and guided by a sense of divine purpose. When blocked, we may feel lost, cynical, or spiritually disconnected.

## Signs of Balance

- Deep spiritual connection and universal oneness
- Clear understanding of divine purpose
- Inner peace and detachment from material chaos
- Strong connection to divine guidance
- Trust in the flow of life

## Signs of Imbalance

- Spiritual disconnection or abandonment
- Loss of purpose or direction
- Over-attachment to material validation
- Dogmatic thinking or spiritual superiority
- Physical symptoms: headaches, dizziness, trouble concentrating

## Root Causes of Imbalance

These often stem from spiritual disconnection, apathy, or trauma around faith and purpose.

- **Disconnection from Source** – Feeling separate from divine presence
  - *Causes:* Loss of faith, unworthiness, lack of spiritual practice
- **Cynicism** – Rejecting spirituality as false or irrelevant
  - *Causes:* Religious trauma, disillusionment, logical over-reliance

- **Spiritual Apathy** – Disinterest in spiritual growth
  - *Causes:* Burnout, emotional numbness, prioritizing material gain
- **Feeling Lost** – Lack of clarity or purpose
  - *Causes:* Life transitions, disconnection from meaning
- **Meaninglessness** – Feeling life has no deeper significance
  - *Causes:* Existential crises, chronic disillusionment

## Ways to Restore Balance

- **Crown meditation:** Visualize a radiant violet or white light pouring into the crown
- **Affirmations:** "I am one with divine wisdom. I trust the path unfolding before me."
- **Spiritual connection practices:** Prayer, stillness, sacred ritual
- **Sekhem energy healing:** Place hands at the crown and channel divine energy
- **Nourish spiritually and physically:** Light fasting, herbal teas, pure water
- **Sacred connection tools:** Symbols of Amun-Ra, meditation under the sky, connecting with silence

By restoring this center, we return to **divine unity and spiritual purpose**. We align with cosmic intelligence and recognize that we are divine beings in human form—anchored in truth, led by light.

## Ways to Restore Balance
## (Seventh Sacred Energy Center)

To strengthen and realign the Seventh Sacred Energy Center, one can:

- **Practice meditation and stillness:** Sit in silence, focusing on breath and divine connection.

- **Use affirmations:** "I am one with the divine. I trust in the wisdom of the universe."

- **Engage in prayer and sacred invocations:** Call upon Amun-Ra or the higher self for divine guidance.

- **Work with Sekhem energy:** Visualize a radiant white or violet light descending from the cosmos into the crown.

- **Nourish the body with high-vibration foods:** Fresh fruits, herbal teas, and fasting practices help maintain spiritual clarity.

- **Incorporate sacred symbols and deities:** Meditate on the Ankh (symbol of eternal life) or the radiant sun disk to embody divine connection.

By restoring balance to this energy center, we awaken our full divine potential, embody spiritual enlightenment, and align with the eternal wisdom of Ma'at. Through this connection, we transcend limitations, embrace divine purpose, and walk as reflections of the divine on Earth.

# THE EIGHTH SACRED ENERGY CENTER: THE REALM OF ANCESTRAL WISDOM AND SPIRITUAL LEGACY

The Eighth Sacred Energy Center governs our connection to ancestral wisdom, spiritual inheritance, and the unseen realms. In Kemet, this center was linked to **Anpu (Anubis)**, the guardian of the gateway between the physical and spiritual worlds. Anpu was revered as the guide who assisted souls in navigating the journey beyond the material plane, ensuring alignment with Ma'at in both life and the afterlife.

Located just above the crown of the head, this energy center serves as a bridge between the personal self and the collective wisdom of those who came before us. The ancient Kemetians understood that life extended beyond the physical realm and that the ancestors continued to play a role in guiding, protecting, and teaching the living.

When this energy center is in balance, we feel a deep sense of purpose, guided by the knowledge that we are part of a lineage that stretches beyond time. We recognize that we do not walk this path alone but with the support of those who came before us. When blocked, we may feel disconnected from our roots, lost in identity, or unable to access ancestral wisdom.

## SIGNS OF BALANCE

- A strong connection to ancestral guidance and spiritual heritage
- Deep intuition and trust in the wisdom of the unseen realms
- A sense of purpose and belonging within a greater lineage
- The ability to receive messages through dreams, divination, or meditation
- Reverence for lineage, history, and cultural traditions

## Signs of Imbalance

- Disconnection from cultural or ancestral roots
- Lack of direction or purpose
- Difficulty accessing intuition or spiritual messages
- Fear of death or the unknown
- Unresolved ancestral trauma or burdens

## Root Causes of Imbalance

- **Feeling Lost** – A deep sense of disorientation or uncertainty about one's place in the world.
  - *Causes:* Cultural erasure, disconnection from lineage.
- **Spiritual Stagnation** – Feeling unable to progress spiritually.
  - *Causes:* Avoidance of ancestral healing, spiritual fatigue.
- **Identity Crisis** – Struggling to define oneself.
  - *Causes:* Colonization, assimilation, disconnection from heritage.
- **Fear of the Unknown** – Anxiety about uncharted spiritual or personal territory.
  - *Causes:* Generational trauma, fear-based beliefs.
- **Inner Conflict** – Conflicting parts of the self causing distress.
  - *Causes:* Suppressed identity, cultural fragmentation.

## Ways to Restore Balance

- **Honor the ancestors:** Create an altar, offer food, water, or incense.
- **Use affirmations:** "I am connected to my ancestors. Their wisdom flows through me."
- **Practice ancestral meditation or dreamwork:** Ask for guidance in dreams and journal insights.
- **Utilize divination tools:** Cowrie shells, tarot, scrying.
- **Work with Sekhem energy:** Visualize a silver or gold light linking to ancestral realms.
- **Eat grounding, memory-enhancing foods:** Roots, greens, mugwort, gotu kola.
- **Invoke sacred symbols and deities:** Meditate on Anpu or carry symbolic representations.

By restoring balance here, we embrace our heritage and divine legacy, accessing ancestral guidance and protection.

## THE NINTH SACRED ENERGY CENTER: THE SEAT OF LIFE FORCE AND VITALITY

The Ninth Sacred Energy Center represents the pinnacle of spiritual awareness and cosmic consciousness. In Kemet, it was associated with **Neberdjer**, the limitless divine source from which all life flows. Neberdjer symbolizes infinite potential, divine intelligence, and oneness with the universe.

Located just above the physical body, this center opens the gateway to the **Amenta** — the field of divine potential. Enlightenment in Kemet wasn't simply personal elevation; it was merging with Ma'at to become a living embodiment of cosmic order and divine will.

When balanced, we feel at peace, connected, and aligned with our sacred mission. When blocked, we may experience disconnection, isolation, or existential despair.

## Signs of Balance

- Unity with all creation
- Peace and spiritual clarity
- Manifestation of divine will
- Access to higher wisdom
- Embodiment of love, truth, and harmony

## Signs of Imbalance

- Feeling spiritually lost or isolated
- Ego over-identification and stagnation
- Resistance to change or growth
- Existential crisis or meaninglessness
- Physical symptoms: headaches, dizziness, energetic heaviness

## Root Causes of Imbalance

- **Fear of the Unknown** – Anxiety about death or uncertainty
  - *Causes:* Survival fears, control, ancestral trauma

- **Existential Dread** – Despair about life's meaning
  - *Causes:* Disillusionment, spiritual crisis
- **Disconnection from Divine Flow** – Inability to trust life
  - *Causes:* Trauma, emotional blocks
- **Nihilism** – Belief that life is meaningless
  - *Causes:* Prolonged suffering, loss of faith
- **Inability to Surrender** – Resistance to divine flow
  - *Causes:* Betrayals, fear of powerlessness
- **Loss of Meaning** – Feeling purposeless
  - *Causes:* Cultural disconnection, prolonged grief
- **Fear of Mortality** – Anxiety about death
  - *Causes:* Lack of grounding, fear of afterlife
- **Isolation** – Detachment from humanity or the divine
  - *Causes:* Rejection of spiritual connection, withdrawal

## Ways to Restore Balance

- **Cosmic meditation:** Visualize merging with the infinite cosmos.
- **Affirmations:** "I am one with the Creator. My consciousness is infinite."
- **Surrender practices:** Let go of control and trust divine guidance.
- **Sekhem energy work:** Channel white or gold light through the crown.

- **Practice sacred stillness:** Connect with nature to observe divine design.

- **Invoke symbols of Neberdjer:** Meditate on the formless divine essence.

By aligning with this center, we live as vessels of divine consciousness, manifesting Ma'at in every thought, word, and action.

## INTEGRATION: PRACTICAL APPLICATIONS OF THE 9 SACRED ENERGY CENTERS

Understanding the 9 Sacred Energy Centers is just the beginning. Transformation happens through living this wisdom. For the Kemetians, balance was not a destination but a daily practice rooted in sacred intention and alignment with Ma'at.

This section will guide you in integrating the energy centers into your life so that Sekhem energy flows harmoniously through your being. As you do, you reclaim your divine identity, awaken ancestral gifts, and become a conscious co-creator of your healing.

### DAILY PRACTICES FOR ENERGY ALIGNMENT

**Morning Rituals**

- **Sekhem breathing:** Slow, intentional breath to activate life force

- **Earthing:** Stand barefoot on the ground to root into stability

- **Affirmations:** Speak one for the energy center you're focusing on (e.g., "I stand in my power")

**Midday Alignment Techniques**

- **Conscious Breathwork:** Pause and breathe deeply, directing awareness to any energy center that feels tense or imbalanced.

- **Creative Movement:** Engage in Kemetic Yoga or dance to activate the Second Sacred Energy Center and keep energy fluid.

- **Structured Water:** Drink water infused with intention, herbs, or crystals to support cellular and energetic alignment.

**Evening Practices for Energy Restoration**

- **Reflect on the Day:** Review emotional experiences and identify which energy centers were activated or blocked.

- **Ritual Bathing:** Take a bath with essential oils, herbs, and sacred intentions to clear energetic residue.

- **Prayer and Meditation:** Close the day by calling on ancestral wisdom through the Eighth Sacred Energy Center.

## ENERGY HEALING TECHNIQUES USING THE KEMETIC CODE™

Healing is the process of realigning with divine order. The following practices support the identification and clearing of blockages within the 9 Sacred Energy Centers:

### SELF-ENERGY SCANNING

Close your eyes, breathe deeply, and mentally scan your body from the base of the spine to the crown. Notice areas of tension. Use intuition or muscle testing to identify blockages.

## Sekhem Energy Activation

Place hands over the energy center needing attention and visualize golden Sekhem light filling the area. Intend harmony and allow the energy to flow naturally.

## Sacred Sound Healing

Use the chant "Sa Sekhem Sahu" (meaning "Divine Life Force Awakening") to clear stagnation and activate Sekhem energy.

## Herbs and Crystals for Support

Each center resonates with specific herbs and crystals:

- **Sixth Energy Center:** Blue lotus for vision
- **Third Energy Center:** Carnelian for personal power

# Developing Your Own Healing Practice

Healing is intuitive and deeply personal. The Kemetic Code™ empowers you to be the master of your own energy.

## Regular Energy Assessment

Notice patterns in your emotions and body. Journaling can help you track which centers require attention.

## Personalized Rituals

Combine movement, Sekhem energy work, affirmations, and sound healing in a way that suits your needs.

## Energy-Aligned Diet

Choose foods that resonate with specific centers:

- **Fourth Center (Heart):** Leafy greens
- **First Center (Root):** Nuts, seeds, root vegetables

## Recognizing Patterns & Long-Term Healing

Healing is a journey of deep awareness and alignment.

## Recognize Recurring Blockages

If certain issues repeatedly show up, a Sacred Energy Center may need long-term attention.

## Seek Support

While self-healing is powerful, working with a trained Kemetic energy practitioner can deepen insight.

## Commit to Spiritual Practice

Energy healing is a way of life. Embrace continuous growth, learning, and self-discovery.

By integrating these practices, we access divine power, restore ancestral wisdom, and embody Ma'at in every aspect of life.

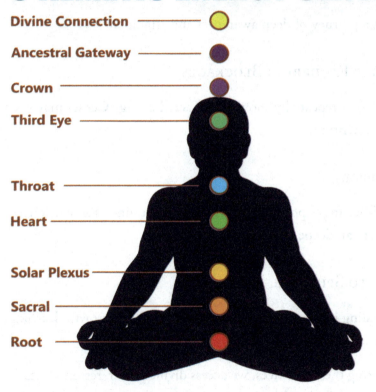

# Chapter 4:
## Applying Energy Healing to Daily Life

*"To know yourself is the beginning of all wisdom."*
— Inscription from the Temple of Luxor, Kemet

### Merging Ancient Wisdom with Modern Understanding

The 9 Sacred Energy Centers are not just ancient philosophy—they offer a living system of healing. The Kemetic Code™ merges this timeless wisdom with modern applications.

Long before Kemet, civilizations like **Kush, Nubia, and Sudan** practiced energy medicine and natural healing. Their knowledge affirms that healing is not new—it is ancestral.

Today, **quantum physics** affirms what our ancestors knew: all matter is energy. Studies in **biofields and neuroscience** confirm that energy impacts health and consciousness (Barušs, 2018; Rubik et al., 2015).

This chapter shows how The Kemetic Code™ bridges ancient tradition with modern energy practices—including the power of **forgiveness** as a key to releasing energy knots and restoring divine balance.

## The Kemetic Code™ Approach to Energy Healing

Healing is not simply "positive thinking." It is structured energetic work that includes:

- **Assessing Energy Centers:** Identifying blockages (Knots) via muscle testing and awareness.

- **Clearing Knots:** Using Sekhem energy, vibration, movement, and affirmations.

- **Maintaining Daily Balance:** Applying rituals, breathwork, and sacred intention.

When practiced consistently, this becomes a powerful tool for health, clarity, and spiritual evolution.

## Step 1: Assessing Your Energy Centers

Before healing can happen, identify where Knots are stored. This is done through muscle testing and intuitive scanning (explained in detail in Chapter 5).

One common blockage to address is the **Forgiveness Knot.**

### Forgiveness and Energy Knots

The Forgiveness Knot is an emotional blockage that stems from unresolved pain or betrayal. It affects multiple energy centers and causes both emotional and physical tension.

## Signs of a Forgiveness Knot:

- Replaying past hurt or injustice
- Emotional stagnation
- Physical tension or fatigue
- Difficulty moving on

Identifying this Knot is the first step to releasing it.

## Step 2: Clearing Knots and Restoring Flow

### 1. Sekhem Energy Healing

Sekhem is life force energy. With focused intention, you can activate it to release emotional blockages.

### Forgiveness Energy Release Technique

1. Place hands over the heart.
2. Inhale golden light into your chest.
3. Chant "Sa Sekhem Sahu" three times.
4. Visualize pain leaving as smoke that transforms and dissipates.

### 2. Vibrational Healing: Mantras

Sound influences brainwaves and promotes healing (Frohlich & McCormick, 2010).

## Forgiveness Mantras

- "I release the weight of this pain. My peace is sacred."
- "Forgiveness is for me, not them. I reclaim my energy."
- "I trust divine justice. I surrender this burden to Ma'at."
- "I am free. I am whole. I am light."

## 3. Kemetic Forgiveness Ritual

**Materials:**

- White candle (purity)
- Bowl of water (cleansing)
- Paper and pen

**Steps:**

1. Light candle and invoke Ma'at.
2. Write down your pain.
3. Read it aloud and declare your release.
4. Submerge the paper in water.
5. Extinguish the candle to seal the ritual.

Repeat as needed until peace is restored.

## STEP 3: MAINTAINING ENERGY ALIGNMENT

Forgiveness unfolds in layers. True release happens when your energy shifts.

### How You Know You've Forgiven:

1. Emotional charge is gone
2. You stop mentally rehearsing the pain
3. No longer seeking revenge or validation
4. You can wish them peace
5. You feel emotionally lighter
6. The pain no longer defines you
7. You set boundaries without guilt
8. You feel more connected to your power

If any feel untrue, the Forgiveness Knot may still be active. Deeper healing or additional Kemetic Code™ work can help.

## SELF-REFLECTION:
## WHERE ARE YOU IN YOUR FORGIVENESS JOURNEY?

- What aspects of this situation have I fully released?
- Where do I still feel tension, guilt, or emotional weight?
- Am I struggling with boundaries, trust, or reclaiming my power?
- What further healing or energy work do I need to move forward?

Forgiveness is not about rushing—it's about honoring your healing at its own pace. Continue clearing Knots as they arise and allow forgiveness to unfold in divine timing. Healing is a practice, not a one-time event. Ongoing forgiveness helps prevent new Knots from forming.

### Evening Forgiveness Reflection

Before sleep, ask yourself:

- Did I hold onto any resentment today?
- Is there someone (including myself) I need to forgive?
- How did I honor balance and truth today?

Write down any lingering emotions and do a brief breathwork practice to prevent energy from stagnating overnight.

## Case Study: Azura's Journey to Forgiveness & Self-Liberation

Azura and her husband suffered a devastating loss—their first child, carried for seven months, did not survive. Instead of grieving together, her husband withdrew in silence. When she became pregnant again, the same emotional distance returned. Even after apologies, the pattern continued.

Eventually, Azura's heart was heavy with resentment and sorrow. Through holistic healing and The Kemetic Code™, she realized:

- Forgiveness is about liberating the future—not forgetting the past.
- She didn't need her husband to change to reclaim her power.
- Healing meant placing herself at the center of her life.

## Akili's Note

Azura's story mirrors my own. I've carried silent wounds—grief, loss, and the ache of invisibility. Forgiveness wasn't easy, but it was freeing. It wasn't about forgetting—it was about choosing peace over pain. The Kemetic Code™ helped me release emotions I hadn't even realized I was holding. That's when healing began.

## Final Thoughts: Forgiveness as a Gateway to Spiritual Evolution

Forgiveness is one of the most powerful tools in The Kemetic Code™. It's more than letting go—it's reclaiming energy, restoring balance, and creating space for your highest self to emerge.

# Chapter 5:
## Using the Kemetic Code™ & Collective Healing

*"He who learns, teaches."*
— African Proverb

### Healing the Self to Heal the Collective

The Kemetic Code™ begins with personal healing, but its true power lies in its ability to transform the collective. Healing ourselves helps heal our families, communities, and the African diaspora.

In Ancient Kemet, society was built on the principle of Ma'at—balance, harmony, truth, and interconnectedness. Colonization, displacement, and cultural erasure have fractured these connections. But The Kemetic Code™ helps restore ancestral ties and create a new legacy for future generations.

This chapter explores:

- How personal healing leads to collective healing
- The ripple effect of restoring balance in relationships and community
- Using The Kemetic Code™ in group settings, activism, and leadership
- Breaking generational cycles and reclaiming ancestral power

## THE RIPPLE EFFECT OF PERSONAL HEALING

### 1. Healing Extends Beyond the Self

Healing one energy center can transform family dynamics, friendships, and workplaces.

**Example:** A mother healing her First Sacred Energy Center (stability) breaks patterns of fear-based survival, empowering her children to thrive without inherited anxiety.

### 2. The Mirror Effect

People naturally reflect the energy around them. When you radiate peace and balance, others shift, too.

**Example:** Healing the Fourth Sacred Energy Center (love & compassion) encourages others to mirror that love, improving relationships across the board.

## Akili's Note: Before I Had a Name for It

In 2008, before any certifications, I worked with college students—brilliant but burdened. They carried trauma, doubt, and fear. What they needed wasn't fixing—it was space to reflect, be seen, and imagine something different.

That space created healing. I later realized it was energy work. Reflection, love, and permission to shift—it was already happening. Titles came later. Healing began with presence.

## 3. Healing Ancestral Lines

Healing reverberates backward and forward. As we clear trauma, we liberate our ancestors and create a clearer path for those to come.

**Example:** Someone healing the Fifth Sacred Energy Center (truth) breaks cycles of silence and secrecy, allowing future generations to live in authenticity and courage.

## 4. Collective Energy Shifts

Imagine an entire community practicing The Kemetic Code™—meditating, honoring ancestors, and working with Sekhem energy.

**Example:** A group engages in ancestral healing rituals and begins to experience more harmony, prosperity, and resilience.

Through our personal alignment, we raise the collective vibration and inspire transformation.

# Applying The Kemetic Code™ in Community & Leadership

Healing is a spiritual act—and also a revolutionary one. As we heal, we become leaders, showing others the path back to balance.

## Healing Circles & Group Work

- **Lead Healing Circles:** Start with a ritual, guide breathwork or Sekhem activation, and invite reflection.

- **Ancestral Veneration Circles:** Gather sacred symbols, pour libations, speak ancestral names.

- **Group Sekhem Activations:** Visualize golden energy flowing among participants, affirm collective healing.

## Energy Work in Activism & Justice

- **Protect Your Energy:** Before protests or organizing, use golden aura visualizations and grounding practices.

- **Chant for Alignment:** Use "Sekhem Ankh Ma'at Ra" for strength and balance.

- **Recover After Action:** Use breathwork, protective crystals, and group debriefs to release stress.

**Note:** Oppression thrives on energetic disconnection. Spiritual alignment is resistance.

## Lead Energy Workshops

Equip communities with tools to maintain resilience, heal trauma, and stay spiritually rooted in turbulent times.

# Breaking Generational Cycles & Reclaiming Ancestral Power

I once thought generational curses were just bad choices. But when I released an inherited Energy Knot passed from my mother in the womb, I realized—this is deeper. We carry energy, beliefs, and wounds from generations before us.

Many imbalances are inherited. The Kemetic Code™ allows us to identify and clear these patterns, liberating our entire lineage.

By healing ourselves, we don't just change our lives—we change the future. We become the living embodiment of ancestral prayers.

## Recognizing & Healing Generational Knots

- **Inherited Beliefs & Traumas**: Many of the fears, doubts, and limitations we carry were passed down through our ancestors' lived experiences. Some were absorbed in the womb; others came from the cultural environment we were born into.

- **Energy Knots in the Sacred Centers**: Using The Kemetic Code™, we can muscle test and release energy knots that have been carried through generations. These knots often stem from ancestral pain, grief, or unresolved experiences that continue to manifest in our lives.

- **Sacred Rituals for Ancestral Healing**: Honoring and calling upon our ancestors to guide us in removing energy blockages and stepping into our divine power. This includes setting up ancestral altars, making offerings, and engaging in meditation or Sekhem energy work focused on lineage healing.

Through this work, we break the cycle of trauma and activate the cycle of healing, wisdom, and empowerment. What would life look like if healing were second nature—if it were simple?

## Muscle Testing: Unlocking the Body's Innate Wisdom

Muscle testing, also known as applied kinesiology or biofeedback testing, is a technique used to tap into the body's innate intelligence. It allows us to assess imbalances, subconscious beliefs, and energy blockages by measuring the body's neuromuscular response to specific stimuli. This practice is based on the understanding that the body is a complex system of energy and information, constantly interacting with its environment.

At its core, muscle testing is a form of communication with the subconscious mind. While the conscious mind may not always be aware of hidden stressors, past traumas, or energetic imbalances, the body holds a record of these experiences. Muscle testing provides a way to access this stored information and determine what is in alignment with the body's optimal health and balance.

**How Muscle Testing Works** Muscle testing operates on the principle that the body responds differently to truth and alignment versus stress and imbalance. When something is beneficial or congruent with the body's well-being, the nervous system remains strong, and the muscle being tested maintains its strength. When something is harmful or incongruent, the nervous system momentarily weakens, causing the muscle to lose strength.

## Basic Test Procedure

1. **Baseline Strength Test** – Apply light pressure to a muscle (such as the deltoid or finger ring grip) while the person resists. This sets a strength baseline.

2. **Test a Statement or Stimulus** – Introduce a statement, food, or trigger. If beneficial, the muscle stays strong; if not, it weakens.

3. **Interpret the Response** – A weak response reveals a stressor or blockage, guiding you to the area needing healing.

In The Kemetic Code™, we use a refined method of muscle testing to identify and clear Knots—blocked or imbalanced energy patterns disrupting harmony within the body. By identifying where Knots are stored in the 9 Sacred Energy Centers, we can facilitate deep energetic release and restoration.

## Why Muscle Testing is Powerful

- **Bypasses the Conscious Mind** – Accesses the subconscious where deeper emotional and ancestral imprints are held.

- **Provides Instant Biofeedback** – Delivers immediate insight into what strengthens or weakens your energy system.

- **Supports Holistic Healing** – Works across physical, emotional, and spiritual levels.

## Muscle Testing in The Kemetic Code™ We use:

- **Finger Rings Test** – Form a ring with thumb and index finger, test resistance using the opposite hand.

- **Alternating Finger Test** – One hand indicates a "Yes" with strength, the other indicates "No" with weakness.

This refined method aligns with Kemetic wisdom and provides precision in identifying and addressing energy blockages.

## From Awareness to Action

Understanding generational cycles and ancestral insights is the first step. But true transformation comes from action—clearing the Knots that hold us back. The Kemetic Code™ gives us the tools to release these blockages and restore harmony within.

## Ensuring You Are Testable

Before using muscle testing for clearing Knots, you must confirm that you are "testable"—your body's energy is balanced enough to give accurate responses.

## How to Check Testability

1. Perform a simple muscle test using the Finger Rings Test or Alternating Finger Test.

2. Say out loud, "My name is [Your Real Name]." Your muscle should stay strong (Yes).

3. Say, "My name is [A Different Name]." Your muscle should weaken (No).

4. If both test the same, your energy is imbalanced—reset is needed.

## Reset Techniques if You Are Not Testable

- **Hydrate** – Drink water.

- **Ground Yourself** – Stand barefoot, breathe deeply, or visualize roots from your feet.

- **Cross the Midline** – Cross arms over the chest or ankles and wrists.

- **Crown Tap Method** – Tap the crown of the head several times while breathing deeply.

Repeat testability check after resetting.

## How to Identify & Release Energy Knots Using The Kemetic Code™

1. **Understanding Energy Knots** Energy knots are deeply embedded blockages resulting from trauma, generational imprints, or repressed emotions. These disrupt Sekhem energy flow, causing imbalance:

   - **Physically** – Chronic tension, illness with no medical explanation.

   - **Emotionally** – Anxiety, limiting beliefs, unresolved grief.

   - **Spiritually** – Feeling disconnected or stuck.

2. **Locating an Energy Knot**

**Step 1: Muscle Testing** Use the Finger Rings Test:

- Form a ring with thumb and middle finger.

- Ask: "Do I have an energy knot that can be released now?"
- Pull with the other hand's fingers. If the ring breaks, the answer is Yes.

This helps identify where energy is blocked so healing can begin.

**Alternating Finger Test:** Form two interlocking rings using your fingers—typically, the thumb and middle finger of one hand form a ring, while the thumb and middle finger of the other hand form a second ring inside the first.

Apply gentle pressure to keep both rings connected while maintaining a relaxed grip.

Ask a yes/no question related to the energy being tested.

Test for a "Yes" response by pulling slightly on the rings. If the response is yes, one of the rings will weaken or break apart easily.

Test for a "No" response by repeating the process. If the response is no, the other ring will weaken or break apart instead.

*Note: When I test, my right-hand ring breaks for a "yes," and my left-hand ring breaks for a "no."*

This technique can be personalized. Pay attention to your body's unique response, and once you identify which ring responds to "yes" and "no," use that method consistently during your energy healing sessions.

Could be a "Yes" or "No" based on your body

## Locating the Specific Energy Center:

Ask aloud or silently: *"Is this energy knot stored in Sacred Center #1?"* Perform a muscle test. If the response is "no," continue sequentially through each center until you receive a "yes" response.

## Step 2: Tune Into Body Awareness & Emotional Triggers

- Scan your body for areas of tension, discomfort, or chronic pain.
- Notice recurring negative thoughts or emotional patterns.
- Pay attention to dreams, ancestral messages, or intuitive nudges pointing to unresolved energy.

## Step 3: The Process of Releasing an Energy Knot

1. **Set Your Intention**

   State: *"I am ready to release what no longer serves me and restore divine balance within."*

   Honor this as a sacred act—clearing energy to make room for Sekhem healing and renewal.

2. **Activate Sekhem Energy**

   Visualize golden light descending from the cosmos and flowing through your entire being.

   Feel it gathering in the identified Sacred Energy Center, gently dissolving any stuck or dense energy.

3. **Clear the Knot**

    - Use your dominant hand to swipe 9 times over the affected center or corresponding area of the body.

    - With each swipe, repeat a Kemetic affirmation such as:

        - *"Sekhem Ankh Ma'at Ra"* (Life force, truth, divine light restore me)

        - *"I release all that is not mine. I return to divine harmony."*

4. **Test for Release**

    Repeat your muscle testing to confirm if the knot has cleared.

    If resistance remains, repeat the process up to three times, then rest and revisit later.

5. **Integrate & Stabilize**

    - Drink water to support energetic processing.

    - Ground yourself—stand barefoot on the earth or meditate for five minutes.

    - Practice calming breathwork to stabilize your system.

    - Journal any emotional or spiritual insights received during the process.

## STEP 4: TRACKING PROGRESS & KNOWING WHEN TO GO DEEPER

Healing unfolds in layers. Some knots clear easily; others require more time and care.

Watch for:

- Emotional patterns or physical symptoms returning—this may signal additional layers needing release.

- New clarity, emotional lightness, or spiritual breakthroughs—these are signs of integration.

- Persistent discomfort—wait 3–7 days, then repeat the process if needed.

By consistently applying The Kemetic Code™, you realign with your divine power, restore ancestral wisdom, and return to balance in mind, body, and spirit.

## Moving Forward: Collective Upliftment & Spiritual Revolution

The Kemetic Code™ is more than a personal healing tool—it is a sacred technology for collective liberation. When we apply these teachings to ourselves, families, and communities, we elevate the collective vibration of the African diaspora. The time to heal is now—and the power to do so is already within us.

# Chapter 6:
## Maintaining Energy Mastery & Long-Term Spiritual Evolution

*"The wise create, while the foolish consume."*
— African Proverb

Healing is not a one-time event—it is an ongoing journey of growth, balance, and spiritual refinement. Once we've cleared energy knots and restored harmony within the 9 Sacred Energy Centers, the next phase is learning how to **maintain** this alignment.

The **Kemetic Code™** is not just a healing technique—it is a **lifestyle**, a sacred commitment to divine order, ancestral power, and conscious evolution.

In this chapter, we will explore:

- **Sustaining Energetic Alignment**: Daily and weekly practices that keep your energy flowing freely.

- **Making The Kemetic Code™ a Lifelong Path**: Deepening your spiritual discipline and intuitive connection.

- **Recognizing Realignment Cues**: Learning to identify when your energy field needs clearing or recalibration.

## Sustaining Energetic Alignment

Maintaining the flow of Sekhem energy requires **discipline**, **awareness**, and **devotion**. Below are foundational tools to help you stay aligned and prevent new energy knots from forming:

### Daily & Weekly Practices for Energy Maintenance

- **Morning Energy Check-In**:

  Upon waking, gently scan your energy centers and ask, *"Where do I feel open? Where is there tension or resistance?"*

- **Sekhem Breathing Ritual**:

  Inhale deeply through the nose, exhale through the mouth, and visualize golden light activating each energy center.

- **Grounding Practices**:

  Stand barefoot on the earth, sit beneath a tree, or engage in Kemetic Yoga postures to root your energy.

- **Journaling & Self-Reflection**:

  Track emotional patterns, insights, dreams, and intuitive downloads. Your journal becomes a mirror of your healing.

- **Sacred Sound Healing**:

  Chant *"Sa Sekhem Sahu"* or other Kemetic mantras to realign your energy field.

- **Regular Energy Clearing**:

  Perform a self-scan at least once a week and use the 9-swipe technique to clear lingering knots.

## RECOGNIZING EARLY SIGNS OF ENERGY IMBALANCE

Energy misalignment often whispers before it screams. Stay attuned to the subtle cues:

- Persistent fatigue or brain fog
- Unusual tension in a specific body part
- Sudden mood changes, irritability, or anxiety
- Feeling spiritually disconnected or uninspired
- Recurring negative thoughts or emotional spirals

Early intervention prevents deeper blocks.

## THE KEMETIC CODE™ AS A LIFELONG PRACTICE

The journey doesn't stop at healing—it expands into **mastery**. Here's how to live The Kemetic Code™ as a daily spiritual path:

## Real-Life Integration of The Kemetic Code™

1. At Work:

   Set energetic intentions before meetings. Use Sekhem breathing for clarity and stay grounded in truth, especially during challenges.

2. In Relationships:

   Practice conscious communication aligned with Ma'at. Use energy awareness to navigate emotional triggers with compassion.

3. In Creativity:

   Channel Sekhem energy into art, writing, business planning, or problem-solving. Creativity is a divine force.

4. In Self-Care:

   Build routines that include energy clearing, Kemetic Yoga, affirmations, nature walks, and sacred baths.

## Attuning to Cycles & Seasons

Ancient Kemetians aligned with nature's rhythms. You can too:

- **Lunar Phases**:

  Use the **waxing moon** to set intentions, and the **waning moon** to release energy knots.

- **Solstices & Equinoxes**:

  Honor seasonal transitions with rituals for recalibration and reflection.

- **Ancestral Timelines**:

  Celebrate the birth and transition anniversaries of ancestors to strengthen spiritual guidance.

## Knowing When to Begin Another Healing Cycle

You may feel called to revisit healing when:

- Old symptoms resurface or new challenges arise
- You feel stagnant or spiritually "off"
- Dreams or synchronicities guide you to deeper work
- You sense a new layer of purpose wanting to emerge

This is not regression—it is **evolution**. Healing happens in **spirals**, not straight lines.

## Making The Kemetic Code™ a Way of Life

To fully embody this path, begin by making these questions and actions part of your daily rhythm:

- **Daily Alignment Check-In**:

  *"Am I living in alignment with Ma'at today?"*

- **Honor Ancestral Wisdom**:

  Maintain altars, offer prayers, and listen for spiritual guidance.

- **Create Sacred Rituals**:

  Engage in practices that keep Sekhem energy flowing—ritual baths, journaling, movement, and meditation.

- **Recognize New Knots as They Surface:**

  Commit to continuous self-inquiry and be willing to return to the healing process.

- **Expand Your Connection to Sekhem:**

  Learn advanced techniques, teach others, and deepen your intuitive trust.

## Akili Note: Stillness Is Not My Assignment

There are days I want to check out—to lay low, to return to unconsciousness. It's tempting, because unconsciousness is simple. You just live at the surface: work, bills, family, repeat. But once you've awakened, you can't unsee.

You feel the pull to rise—not just for yourself, but for your people.

You feel the pain of the collective.

You start asking bigger questions.

And when I feel tired, I listen for the voice of my higher self. I remember:

**I am not built for stillness.**

Yes, I rest. Yes, I pause. But I am here to **shift the vibration** of this world.

I am a **different kind of revolutionary**. A healer. A mirror. A culture-bearer.

And **culture is the medicine.**

# Final Thoughts: Mastery Is a Journey, Not a Destination

Mastery doesn't mean perfection. It means becoming deeply attuned to your energy, your purpose, and your divine power.

It means choosing awareness over avoidance.

It means returning to alignment, again and again.

It means embodying what your ancestors lived, died, and dreamed for.

By walking this path, you are restoring sacred knowledge, realigning with your divine self, and building a spiritual legacy for the generations to come.

# CHAPTER 7:
## Embodying the Kemetic Code™ & Elevating Collective Consciousness

---

"When there is no enemy within, the enemy outside can do you no harm." – African Proverb Healing and spiritual alignment are not meant to be temporary efforts—they are meant to be embodied. The Kemetic Code™ is a way of being. It shapes how we move through the world, how we connect with others, and how we elevate the collective consciousness of our people.

In this chapter, we explore how to fully integrate The Kemetic Code™ into your life, step into energetic leadership, and contribute to the spiritual awakening of the African diaspora.

### Living in Alignment with The Kemetic Code™

#### Self-Reflection: Recognizing Your Alignment

Alignment is not perfection—it is presence. When you're truly flowing with The Kemetic Code™, your energy, choices, and emotions reflect a deeper awareness and trust. Reflect with the following questions:

- Do I feel ease and clarity in my daily actions, or do I feel resistance and struggle?

- Am I making choices from divine wisdom, or reacting from fear and habit?

- When faced with challenges, do I lean into my spiritual tools, or do I disconnect from them?

- Do my relationships reflect mutual respect, balance, and truth?

- Am I guided by intuition, or am I seeking validation from others?

If any of these reveal misalignment, it's not failure—it's an invitation to come back into balance. This is the moment where practice becomes embodiment.

## From Practice to Embodiment

- Instead of "practicing Ma'at," you embody balance and truth in all you do.

- Instead of "doing energy work," you become a vessel for Sekhem energy to flow naturally.

- Instead of "seeking wisdom," you live in communion with ancestral knowing.

This shift requires trust in your inner voice. It is the knowing that The Kemetic Code™ is not something you do—it becomes who you are.

## ENERGY LEADERSHIP & EXPANDING YOUR IMPACT

### SIGNS YOU ARE READY FOR ENERGY LEADERSHIP

You don't choose energy leadership—it chooses you as you evolve. You'll know you're stepping into it when:

- People begin to seek your presence and guidance.
- You feel called to share—not from ego, but from service.
- You detach from outcomes and trust others' timing.
- You embody compassion more than urgency.

Leadership doesn't require a stage or a title. Some lead quietly in their households. Others lead by mentoring or simply radiating calm. Honor the way you naturally uplift others.

### GUIDING WITHOUT FORCING

- Lead by example—your frequency speaks louder than your words.
- Honor free will—some may not be ready, and that's okay.
- Share only when invited—offer wisdom, don't impose it.

### AVOIDING BURNOUT AS A LEADER

- Set healthy boundaries—every call is not yours to answer.
- Cleanse your energy field—use meditation, Sekhem breathwork, or sound healing.
- Prioritize solitude—leaders need space to recharge.

## Energetic Discernment

- Know when to hold space.
- Know when to protect your field.
- Let intuition guide your engagement.

## Entrepreneurial Leadership & Building Black Legacy

### The Role of Ownership in Spiritual Sovereignty

Entrepreneurship is more than income—it is spiritual sovereignty. For centuries, our people were denied financial autonomy. Ownership is revolutionary.

When we build and control our platforms, we shift power. When we align business with Ma'at—truth, balance, justice—we don't just succeed personally—we empower our people.

### Aligning Business with Spiritual Purpose

Spirituality and business are not separate—they are partners in purpose. To keep your work aligned:

- Practice service-based leadership: Build businesses that uplift others.
- Practice ethical wealth-building: Reject exploitation, dishonesty, and imbalance.
- Infuse your business with spiritual practice: Use intentions, rituals, and alignment in your workflow.

## Building Generational Wealth

Generational wealth goes beyond money—it's about passing on values, knowledge, and opportunity. Start by:

- Learning financial literacy and investing wisely.
- Prioritizing ownership over consumption.
- Teaching the next generation about sovereignty, balance, and creation.

## Spiritual Leadership in Business

A spiritually aligned business:

- Operates ethically.
- Serves the community.
- Reflects divine purpose.

# Becoming a Certified Kemetic Code™ Practitioner

For those called to guide others, becoming a Certified Kemetic Code™ Practitioner may be your next step.

You will:

- Deepen your knowledge of Sekhem energy, muscle testing, and energy clearing.
- Facilitate transformation in others and support your community.

- Join a global network of energy leaders restoring Ma'at and ancestral power.

Visit **KemeticCode.com** to begin your practitioner journey.

## Akili Note

There was a time I never imagined offering this kind of healing system—one rooted in our ancestral brilliance—for the world to use.

For so long, I thought healing was something I had to do alone, in silence. I didn't know my liberation would become a lighthouse for others.

It wasn't ego that pushed me—it was urgency. I saw the heaviness in our people. I felt it. And I knew we already held the answers.

There is a shift happening. I feel it. Many of us do. A collective rising.

Not one built on control, but on balance. Not on domination, but on harmony.

The Kemetic Code™ is my offering—but it is not mine alone. I am one of many remembering, rising, and answering the call.

## Final Reflections: Becoming the Living Code

When you truly embody The Kemetic Code™, it stops being a method—it becomes your essence.

Your thoughts, your breath, your presence begin to carry the frequency of divine alignment. You live as a vessel of Sekhem. You radiate Ma'at. You become the living code.

This journey will continue through you—through the people you heal, the children you raise, the communities you build, and the ancestors who walk with you.

You are not just learning the code.

**You are The Kemetic Code™.**

# Chapter 8:
## Trusting Your Path & Embracing Future Evolution

*"To return to the source is to find meaning."*
– African Proverb

Spiritual mastery is not about reaching a final destination—it is an ever-unfolding journey of growth, expansion, and transformation. The Kemetic Code™ is not a static practice; it evolves with you as you deepen your awareness, face new challenges, and expand into greater spiritual wisdom. This chapter explores how to embrace continuous evolution, deepen your ancestral connection, and trust the divine unfolding of your spiritual path.

## Embracing Evolution as a Lifelong Practice

### The Ever-Unfolding Path

Unlike rigid spiritual systems, The Kemetic Code™ is fluid—it grows as you grow. Your spiritual needs will shift over time, requiring adaptability and openness. Embracing evolution means allowing yourself to:

- **Release Old Identities** – Who you were at the start of this journey is not who you are becoming. Let go of labels or practices that no longer serve you.

- **Remain Open to New Wisdom** – As you deepen your understanding, new layers of truth will emerge. Be willing to expand beyond what you currently know.

- **Trust the Seasons of Growth** – Some phases require deep inner work, while others call for outward action. Trust the rhythm of your spiritual expansion.

## Aligning with Your Evolving Purpose

Purpose is not a fixed destination—it refines itself over time. Your role within The Kemetic Code™ will shift as you integrate new levels of wisdom. Ask yourself:

- How has my understanding of my purpose expanded?

- What aspects of The Kemetic Code™ feel most alive for me right now?

- How can I allow my spiritual practice to align with where I am today?

## Ancestral Veneration: Strengthening the Connection

Honoring the ancestors is a foundational aspect of Kemetic spiritual practice. Our ancestors are not gone; they are guides, protectors, and sources of wisdom who continue to influence our journey. By fostering a relationship with them, we anchor ourselves in the continuum of divine knowledge that has been passed down through generations.

## Creating an Ancestral Altar

An ancestral altar serves as a sacred space to honor and communicate with those who came before us. To set up an altar:

- **Choose a Dedicated Space** – A quiet, undisturbed location where you can consistently connect.

- **Include Essential Elements**:

  - Photographs or symbolic representations of your ancestors.

  - A glass of water to serve as a conduit between realms.

  - Candles to represent light and guidance.

  - Incense or herbs such as frankincense or myrrh to purify the space.

  - Offerings of food, flowers, or personal items connected to your lineage.

## Types of Offerings & Their Meanings

- **Water** – Purification, communication, and a bridge between worlds.

- **Food** – Nourishment for the spirit, often items your ancestors enjoyed.

- **Incense & Herbs** – Spiritual cleansing, elevation, and protection.

- **Written Prayers & Letters** – A direct way to express gratitude, seek guidance, or share your intentions.

## PRAYERS & INVOCATIONS FOR ANCESTOR CONNECTION

- **Prayer of Gratitude:**

"Ancestors of my bloodline and spirit, I honor you. I give thanks for your wisdom, strength, and sacrifices. May your guidance continue to illuminate my path. May I walk in alignment with the foundation you have laid. Ase."

- **Prayer for Guidance:**

"Ancient ones, I seek your counsel. Speak to me through dreams, signs, and intuition. Reveal to me what I must learn and how I must grow. I listen with an open heart and honor your presence in my life. Ase."

## HOW TO INTERPRET ANCESTRAL MESSAGES

- **Dreams** – Pay attention to recurring themes, symbols, or direct communication from ancestors.

- **Synchronicities** – Repeated numbers, unexpected encounters, or messages that feel significant.

- **Intuitive Knowing** – A deep sense of clarity or an urge to take specific actions.

## Daily & Periodic Rituals to Maintain Connection

- **Morning or Evening Offerings** – Pour a libation (a small amount of water or wine) while speaking their names.

- **Journaling & Reflection** – Write down messages, insights, or gratitude to your ancestors.

- **Celebrating Ancestral Days** – Honoring birthdays, anniversaries, or traditional spiritual festivals that align with your lineage.

## Akili Note

There are moments on this journey when I feel like I've barely scratched the surface—and others when I'm in awe of how far I've come. That's the beauty of spiritual evolution: it doesn't rush you. It unfolds in layers. Sometimes loud. Sometimes still.

I've learned to honor the quiet rituals—my tea, my journal, a whispered question to my ancestors. I tune in with my pendulum, pull a card, or just sit in silence and feel. That's where my guidance lives. That's where my strength returns.

I don't always know where this path is leading, but I trust it. I trust the nudges. I trust the pauses. I trust that even when it's not clear, I am not lost. I am guided. And I am growing.

Let this chapter remind you: your path is sacred, even when it's soft. Especially when it's soft.

## Personal Visioning: Mapping Your Spiritual Future

Your spiritual journey is a living, breathing path—one that continues to unfold as you grow. To fully integrate The Kemetic Code™, take an active role in shaping your spiritual vision.

### Guided Visioning Exercise

Find a quiet space, close your eyes, and take a few deep breaths. Envision yourself five years from now, fully aligned with your spiritual purpose. Ask yourself:

- What does my daily spiritual practice look like?
- How do I embody the principles of The Kemetic Code™ in my relationships, work, and personal growth?
- What feelings arise as I live in alignment with my highest self?
- Write down a personal vision statement that reflects your intentions.

## Symbolic Action: Bringing Your Vision to Life

To anchor your vision in reality:

- Create a vision altar with symbols of your evolving spiritual path.
- Craft a personal mantra affirming your alignment with The Kemetic Code™.
- Write a letter to your future self, describing how you will nurture your spiritual evolution.

## Closing Intention

"I trust my path. I walk in divine alignment. The wisdom of my ancestors, the power of Sekhem, and the balance of Ma'at guide me in all things."

By embracing your unique evolution and honoring your ancestral lineage, The Kemetic Code™ moves through you, guiding you toward greater wisdom, balance, and divine alignment.

# Chapter 9:
## The Power of Energy Healing – Real Stories of Transformation

---

*"Healing is not an event; it is a process."*
— African Wisdom

While scientific studies validate the effectiveness of energy healing, personal experiences bring these practices to life. Here are real accounts of individuals who have experienced profound healing as they embraced energy medicine:

### Case Study 1: From Chronic Pain to Freedom

For years, Monica, a 45-year-old entrepreneur, suffered from chronic migraines and persistent fatigue. Doctors provided medications, but nothing offered lasting relief. Frustrated, she turned to energy healing. Through biofield therapy and Sekhem energy work, she discovered that trapped emotional energy from past trauma was manifesting as physical pain.

She began working with energy clearing techniques, learning how to release blocked emotions stored in her body. Over time, she started noticing subtle changes—her headaches became less frequent, her sleep improved, and she felt more energized throughout the day. After several months of consistent practice, Monica realized that the migraines that had ruled her life were now a rare occurrence. More importantly, she felt emotionally lighter, no longer weighed down by stress and past pain. Energy healing not only freed her from chronic pain but also helped her regain her joy and focus.

## Case Study 2: Overcoming Emotional Trauma

After a painful breakup, Jared, a 33-year-old teacher, struggled with persistent anxiety and emotional numbness. Traditional therapy helped, but something still felt stuck. He began practicing energy clearing techniques, releasing deep-seated knots related to unworthiness and rejection.

The first time he tried clearing energy, he didn't notice much difference. But as he continued, he began feeling moments of unexpected peace—his heart rate would slow, and the tightness in his chest would ease. He realized that his emotional numbness was his body's way of protecting him from unresolved pain. Through daily energy alignment practices, he gradually peeled back the layers of past hurt, allowing himself to feel deeply again without fear. Now, he uses energy healing to maintain emotional balance, and he has cultivated healthier relationships built on trust and self-worth.

## Case Study 3: Healing Beyond Words

Angela, a 52-year-old nonprofit worker, always felt a mysterious sadness she couldn't explain. It wasn't until she explored energy healing that she realized she was carrying ancestral grief passed down through generations. Using energy clearing techniques to remove energy blockages, she not only felt relief but also a deep connection to her lineage.

She experienced vivid dreams of ancestors she had never met and felt emotions that didn't seem to belong to her. Each time she released an energetic blockage, she felt herself growing lighter, more at peace. Through this journey, she recognized that healing herself was also healing the generations before and after her. She now teaches energy healing techniques to her community, ensuring that others have the opportunity to break free from inherited trauma and get to a place of peace.

## Case Study 4: Restoring Balance After Burnout

Tasha, a 38-year-old social worker, constantly put others before herself. Years of emotional exhaustion led to severe burnout, affecting her mental and physical health. Through energy alignment techniques, she learned to restore her energetic balance, set boundaries, and prioritize self-care.

At first, the idea of focusing on herself felt selfish. But as she started practicing energy healing, she realized how much unresolved emotional energy she had been carrying for others. She worked with clearing techniques to release tension from her heart and solar plexus, where she felt the most heaviness. Over time, she felt a shift—less drained at the end of the day, more present in her work, and finally able to set healthy boundaries. Now, she integrates energy healing into her daily routine, ensuring that she nourishes herself so she can continue serving her community.

## Case Study 5: Breaking the Cycle of Generational Trauma

Malik, a 29-year-old entrepreneur, grew up in a family where emotional suppression was the norm. He realized that many of his struggles with confidence stemmed from inherited trauma. Using energy clearing to release deep-rooted knots, he unlocked a newfound self-assurance and broke free from limiting patterns.

The first time he did an energy clearing session, he felt an overwhelming wave of emotion surface—grief, anger, and sadness that he had never allowed himself to process. As he continued clearing, he noticed how much lighter he felt, and his interactions with his family started changing. He became more open, more expressive, and—most importantly—more at peace with himself. His journey encouraged his siblings to start their own healing work, proving that one person's transformation can create ripples through generations.

These diverse stories showcase how energy healing has the potential to transform lives—physically, emotionally, and spiritually. Whether you are seeking relief from stress, healing from trauma, or unlocking new levels of personal growth, energy work can be the key to unlocking your highest potential.

## Case Study 6: Overcoming Social Anxiety

Aisha, a 31-year-old artist, struggled with severe social anxiety that kept her from fully expressing herself. She realized through energy healing that her fear of judgment stemmed from a childhood rejection. Throughout her life, she had developed the habit of shrinking herself to avoid attention, fearing criticism or ridicule.

At first, she was skeptical about energy healing, but after trying a few simple clearing exercises, she began noticing subtle shifts. She committed to regular energy alignment practices, and with each session, she uncovered and released deeply held emotional knots related to past social experiences. Slowly, she became more comfortable sharing her work—first with close friends, then in small art circles.

After several months, she took a bold step—hosting her first art exhibition. Standing in front of an audience, she no longer felt paralyzed by fear. Today, she confidently speaks about her creative process and even mentors other young artists—something she never thought possible.

## Case Study 7: Healing from Chronic Back Pain

James, a 42-year-old fitness coach, suffered from chronic lower back pain for over a decade. Traditional treatments provided only temporary relief, but the pain always returned. It wasn't until he explored energy healing that he realized his physical discomfort was linked to suppressed emotions.

James had always been the strong one in his family, taking on the burdens of others while neglecting his own needs. Through muscle testing and energy clearing, he discovered that the tension in his lower back corresponded to feelings of unworthiness and unresolved childhood fears. He committed to a daily practice of energy clearing and breathwork, releasing emotional knots stored in his body.

Over time, his pain decreased, and for the first time in years, he could move freely without discomfort. More importantly, he felt emotionally lighter and more in tune with his needs. Today, he integrates energy work into his fitness training, helping his clients achieve holistic healing beyond physical strength.

## Case Study 8: Restoring Emotional Balance After Divorce

Tamika, a 39-year-old mother of two, went through a painful divorce that left her emotionally exhausted and disconnected from herself. The heartbreak and betrayal weighed heavily on her, affecting her ability to function day to day. She felt lost, unsure of who she was outside of the marriage.

Desperate for healing, she turned to energy work. In her first few sessions, she uncovered energetic knots related to abandonment and self-worth—many of which had been imprinted long before her marriage. She began a journey of daily energy clearing, learning to separate her identity from the pain she carried.

Over time, the grief lifted, and she started feeling a renewed sense of self. Through journaling, movement, and continued energy alignment, she transformed her perspective—seeing the divorce not as a failure but as a new beginning. Now, Tamika is thriving, co-parenting peacefully, and embracing a future full of possibilities.

## Case Study 9: Releasing Financial Blocks

Shayla, a 35-year-old business owner, struggled with self-sabotage in business due to subconscious beliefs about money. Despite her talent and hard work, she always seemed to hit a plateau, unable to break past a certain income level. No matter how much effort she put into growing her business, something held her back.

Through energy clearing, she discovered that childhood experiences of financial instability had created a deep fear of success. Growing up, she had heard phrases like "money doesn't grow on trees" and "rich people are greedy," which unconsciously shaped her relationship with abundance.

She began working with muscle testing to identify and clear financial blocks, focusing on the emotional knots tied to scarcity. After several months of deep inner work, she noticed a shift—not only in her mindset but in her business. Opportunities she once resisted started flowing easily, and she felt confident in charging what she was worth. Today, Shayla's business is thriving, and she no longer feels guilt or fear around financial success.

## CASE STUDY 10: STRENGTHENING RELATIONSHIPS

David, a 47-year-old husband and father, often felt emotionally distant from his family. He couldn't understand why—despite loving them deeply. His inability to express affection led to strained relationships with his wife and children. He felt trapped in a cycle of emotional detachment but didn't know how to break free.

Through energy healing, David uncovered deep-rooted wounds from childhood, where emotional expression was discouraged. He discovered that his body had stored years of suppressed emotions in his chest and throat, making it physically uncomfortable to communicate his feelings.

He committed to daily energy clearing practices, focusing on releasing these emotional knots. Gradually, he noticed a change—his interactions with his family became warmer, his words more open and heartfelt. Over time, his marriage strengthened, and he developed a deeper bond with his children. Now, he is a firm believer in energy healing, using it to maintain emotional balance and authentic connection with his loved ones.

## CASE STUDY 11: OVERCOMING FEAR OF PUBLIC SPEAKING

Nia, a 26-year-old college student, avoided speaking in public at all costs. Even the thought of introducing herself in a group would cause her heart to race and her palms to sweat. She had spent most of her life hiding in the background, terrified of being judged or embarrassed.

Determined to overcome this fear, Nia turned to energy healing. Through muscle testing and emotional release techniques, she traced her fear back to a childhood incident where she was humiliated in front of her classmates. That single event had created an energy blockage in her throat chakra, preventing her from feeling safe while speaking.

With consistent energy clearing and vocal exercises, she began to release this old fear. The next time she had to speak in class, she still felt nervous—but noticed she could push through the discomfort. With each speaking opportunity, her confidence grew. Eventually, Nia stepped into a leadership role on campus, facilitating discussions and leading presentations with ease. She had transformed from someone who avoided speaking to someone who commanded the room with presence and clarity.

## Case Study 12: Enhancing Athletic Performance

Jordan, a 22-year-old athlete, noticed a pattern of underperforming in high-pressure situations. Despite his skill and training, his body would tense up during competitions, causing him to make mistakes at crucial moments. Coaches told him it was just nerves, but Jordan knew there was something deeper at play.

Seeking an alternative solution, he explored energy healing. Through muscle testing, he identified an energy blockage in his solar plexus, tied to a fear of failure that had been embedded since childhood. His subconscious mind had created a protective mechanism that would trigger tension and self-sabotage whenever he approached a big moment.

By using breathwork, visualization, and energy clearing, Jordan began reprogramming his response to high-pressure situations. Over time, he noticed a shift—his body felt lighter, his mind clearer, and his movements more fluid during competitions. His performance improved significantly, and he went on to win multiple championships. Today, he credits energy healing as a key factor in his athletic success, using it as a tool to keep his mind and body in peak condition.

## Case Study 13: Finding Purpose and Clarity

Sophia, a 50-year-old nonprofit worker, felt lost after her children left home. She had spent decades pouring her energy into raising a family and supporting others, but when she found herself with an empty nest, she struggled to figure out who she was beyond those roles. The sense of purpose that once grounded her had faded, leaving her with feelings of uncertainty and restlessness.

Through energy healing, Sophia began clearing emotional knots related to self-worth and identity. She realized that much of her sense of purpose had been tied to external validation. As she released these blocks, she started to reconnect with the things that once brought her joy—writing, community work, and mentoring young women.

She embraced energy alignment as part of her daily routine, using it to gain clarity and set new intentions for the next phase of her life. Soon, opportunities began appearing—she was invited to lead a mentorship program, helping young women navigate life with confidence. Sophia now feels more fulfilled than ever, knowing that her purpose is not just to serve others but also to honor her own passions and spiritual journey.

## Case Study 14: A Pet's Healing Journey

Kim, a 48-year-old pet owner, noticed her rescue dog, Onyx, suffered from extreme anxiety. He would tremble uncontrollably during thunderstorms, cower in fear around strangers, and refuse to eat when left alone. No amount of training or behavioral therapy seemed to help. Desperate to ease his distress, Kim turned to energy healing.

She began using gentle energy clearing techniques on Onyx, focusing on calming his nervous system and releasing any past trauma stored in his body. At first, he remained tense, but after a few sessions, she noticed subtle changes—his tail wagged a little more, and he began to relax in situations that previously triggered fear.

Over time, his anxiety became less intense, and he started showing signs of trust and confidence. Now, Onyx is a completely different dog. He no longer hides during storms, greets visitors with curiosity instead of fear, and enjoys his daily walks without hesitation. Kim believes energy healing not only helped Onyx recover but also deepened their bond, proving that energetic balance is just as important for animals as it is for humans.

## Akili's Note

As you've seen from these case studies, healing is not just possible—it is your birthright.

Each of these individuals started with one simple decision: to believe in the possibility of change. They committed to showing up for themselves, not perfectly, but consistently. They honored their pain, listened to their bodies, and opened themselves to the energy of transformation.

You don't have to have all the answers. You don't need to be fearless or flawless. You just need to take that first step—to trust that your healing matters, that your life has meaning beyond your wounds.

As you continue your journey with The Kemetic Code™, remember: healing is not linear. Some days you'll feel powerful, and other days you'll feel like you're starting over. Both are part of the process. Give yourself grace.

You are not alone. You are supported by the unseen ancestors, guided by divine intelligence, and surrounded by a community of others on the path. You are more than your trauma. You are a vessel of divine light, capable of creating new realities.

Trust in your power. Commit to your evolution. And remember, healing isn't just something you do—it's who you become.

# Epilogue:
## Becoming the Code

This is not the end of your journey—it's only the beginning. The Kemetic Code™ is not just a system of healing; it's a way of life, a daily invitation to return to your highest self.

As you continue practicing the tools in this book, you will notice shifts—not just in your emotions or energy but in the very way you move through the world. You'll speak with more clarity, love with more depth, and dream with more courage.

You'll begin to notice the sacred in the ordinary: the breath that grounds you, the sunrise that renews you, the ancestors who whisper through your intuition. You'll start to live from a place of intention rather than reaction. And you'll inspire others—not by preaching or persuading, but by the quiet power of your alignment.

Becoming the Code means allowing healing to shape you from the inside out. It means living with integrity, compassion, and purpose. It means remembering that you are not broken—you are brilliant.

So take this wisdom, not as doctrine, but as a mirror. Use it to reflect your light, your truth, your possibility. The world needs your healing, your voice, your vision.

This is your invitation. Your rebirth. Your return to wholeness.

Live it boldly.

1. Commit to Daily Spiritual Alignment

    Your spiritual practice should be a source of strength and renewal. To maintain your connection:

    Begin each day with a Sekhem breathwork practice or Kemetic mantra.

    Perform self-energy scans to check for any imbalances and apply The Kemetic Code™ techniques to realign.

    End the day with an ancestral offering or moment of gratitude to acknowledge divine guidance.

2. Expand Your Knowledge & Practice

    Your understanding of The Kemetic Code™ will deepen as you explore new dimensions of spiritual wisdom. Consider:

    Studying Kemetic texts, philosophy, and meditative practices to strengthen your foundation.

    Exploring Kemetic energy healing techniques beyond what was introduced in this book.

    Engaging in advanced breathwork, sound healing, or vibrational alignment practices.

3. Engage with a Like-Minded Community

   Spiritual growth is accelerated when shared with others. You do not have to walk this path alone. Connect with those who are also on the journey by:

   Joining online and in-person Kemetic spiritual communities to exchange insights and support.

   Attending workshops, retreats, or healing circles to deepen your practice.

   Engaging in ancestral remembrance ceremonies and community rituals to collectively restore our spiritual heritage.

4. Apply The Kemetic Code™ to Every Area of Life

   True mastery is not measured by how much you know but by how well you embody wisdom. Integrate The Kemetic Code™ into:

   Your Relationships – Approach interactions with balance, truth, and harmony.

   Your Career & Work – Operate with integrity, align your work with your purpose, and create impact.

   Your Creativity & Expression – Channel Sekhem energy into art, music, writing, and sacred movement.

## Staying Connected to the Path

This is only the beginning. If you feel called to take your understanding deeper, consider:

Becoming a Certified Kemetic Code™ Practitioner: If you are drawn to facilitating healing for others, practitioner training provides the structure and knowledge to guide others in alignment with The Kemetic Code™.

Exploring Future Offerings: Workshops, advanced training, and mentorship programs are available for those committed to long-term spiritual mastery.

Engaging with the Kemetic Code™ Community: Whether through online forums, live discussions, or group healing sessions, staying connected will ensure continuous growth.

For more resources, visit KemeticCode.com to explore courses, mentorship, and upcoming events.

## Final Affirmation & Blessing

May you walk forward with clarity, knowing that the divine within you is always guiding your steps. May you trust yourself, knowing that your ancestors walk with you.

May you stand in your power, discovering all that was lost, and ensuring that future generations will never have to search for their spiritual inheritance again.

You are The Kemetic Code™.

To honor the wisdom and science that support The Kemetic Code™, the following sources are included to give credit and context to the ideas referenced throughout this work. This list reflects a blend of ancestral reverence and contemporary research, showing that ancient truths and modern science can—and do—coexist.

# Appendix

## The 42 Laws of Ma'at

**Also known as the Negative Confessions or Declarations of Innocence**

- ✓ I have not committed sin.
- ✓ I have not committed robbery with violence.
- ✓ I have not stolen.
- ✓ I have not slain men or women.
- ✓ I have not stolen food.
- ✓ I have not swindled offerings.
- ✓ I have not stolen from God/Goddess.
- ✓ I have not told lies.
- ✓ I have not carried away food.
- ✓ I have not cursed.

- ✓ I have not closed my ears to truth.
- ✓ I have not committed adultery.
- ✓ I have not made anyone cry.
- ✓ I have not felt sorrow without reason.
- ✓ I have not assaulted anyone.
- ✓ I am not deceitful.
- ✓ I have not stolen anyone's land.
- ✓ I have not been an eavesdropper.
- ✓ I have not falsely accused anyone.
- ✓ I have not been angry without reason.
- ✓ I have not seduced anyone's spouse.
- ✓ I have not polluted myself.
- ✓ I have not terrorized anyone.
- ✓ I have not disobeyed the Law.
- ✓ I have not been exclusively angry.
- ✓ I have not cursed God/Goddess.
- ✓ I have not behaved with violence.
- ✓ I have not caused disruption of peace.
- ✓ I have not acted hastily or without thought.
- ✓ I have not overstepped my boundaries of concern.

✓ I have not exaggerated my words when speaking.

✓ I have not worked evil.

✓ I have not used evil thoughts, words, or deeds.

✓ I have not polluted the water.

✓ I have not spoken angrily or arrogantly.

✓ I have not cursed anyone in thought, word, or deed.

✓ I have not placed myself on a pedestal.

✓ I have not stolen what belongs to God/Goddess.

✓ I have not stolen from or disrespected the deceased.

✓ I have not taken food from a child.

✓ I have not acted with insolence.

✓ I have not destroyed property belonging to God/Goddess.

## THE KEMETIC CODE™ SELF-HEALING CHEAT SHEET

### PREPARE

✓ Hydrate

✓ Ground yourself (barefoot or visualize roots)

✓ Set your intention (e.g. "I'm ready to release what no longer serves me.")

### CHECK TESTABILITY

✓ Muscle test "My name is [Real Name]" → Strong = YES

- ✓ "My name is [Fake Name]" → Weak = NO
- ✓ If results are off, reset with: Drink water, Tap crown, Cross arms/ankles

## Identify the Knot

- ✓ Ask: "Do I have an energy knot ready to release now?" → Test
- ✓ If yes, ask: "Is it in Sacred Center #1?" → Test up to #9
- ✓ Confirm the feeling state if known (fear, shame, resentment, etc.)

## Clear the Knot

- ✓ Place your dominant hand over the energy center
- ✓ Visualize golden Sekhem energy flowing in
- ✓ Swipe hand 9 times over the area
- ✓ Repeat: "Sekhem Ankh Ma'at Ra" or "I release all that is not mine. I return to divine harmony."

## Confirm Release

- ✓ Muscle test again: "Is the knot released?"
- ✓ If no, repeat steps or rest and revisit later

## Integrate

- ✓ Drink water
- ✓ Breathe deeply

- ✓ Journal insights
- ✓ Walk barefoot or touch the earth

## TROUBLESHOOTING & COMMON SCENARIOS

| Issue | Possible Cause | What to Do |
|---|---|---|
| I can't tell if the muscle test is working | Nervous system imbalance | Drink water, ground, or use crown tap reset |
| My muscle test gives the same response for "Yes" and "No" | Not testable yet | Reset energy using grounding hydration |
| I don't feel anything during the clearing | Not all knots have a strong sensation | Trust the process; emotional or energetic release isn't always physical |
| I feel emotional afterward | Normal integration response | Journal, rest, breathe, and drink water |
| Knot keeps coming back | Layered or ancestral knot | Repeat gently over days; consider working with a practitioner |
| I don't know which energy center to focus on | Overwhelmed or unclear | Muscle test each center, or start with Root and move upward |
| I feel stuck in my healing journey | Resistance or deeper emotional layer | Step back, offer yourself grace, and revisit when ready |

# WORKS CITED

Asante, Molefi Kete. The Egyptian Philosophers: Ancient African Voices from Imhotep to Akhenaten. African American Images, 2001.

Baruss, Imants, and Julia Mossbridge. Transcendent Mind: Rethinking the Science of Consciousness. American Psychological Association, 2018.

Dispenza, Joe. Breaking the Habit of Being Yourself: How to Lose Your Mind and Create a New One. Hay House, 2012.

Frohlich, F., & McCormick, D. A. "Endogenous Electric Fields May Guide Neocortical Network Activity." Neuron, vol. 67, no. 1, 2010, pp. 129–143.

Lipton, Bruce H. The Biology of Belief: Unleashing the Power of Consciousness, Matter & Miracles. Hay House, 2005.

Ra Un Nefer Amen. Metu Neter, Vol. 1: The Great Oracle of Tehuti and the Egyptian System of Spiritual Cultivation. Khamit Media Transvision, 1990.

Rubik, Beverly, et al. "Biofield Science and Healing: History, Terminology, and Concepts." Global Advances in Health and Medicine, vol. 4, suppl, 2015, pp. 8–14.

Wilson, Amos N. Blueprint for Black Power: A Moral, Political, and Economic Imperative for the Twenty-First Century. Afrikan World Infosystems, 1998.

# ABOUT THE AUTHOR

Akili Worthy is a spiritual teacher, healer, and creator of The Kemetic Code™, a transformational energy healing system rooted in the wisdom of Ancient Kemet and ancestral African traditions. With a Master's in Education and over a decade of experience as both a teacher and a guide, Akili brings a unique fusion of structured learning and sacred wisdom to every space she holds.

Her work is a sacred blend of science, soul, and sovereignty—designed to help people clear the energetic interruptions that block their power, purpose, and peace.

Certified in energy medicine, hypnosis, coaching, and ancestral healing, Akili has helped hundreds reclaim their voice, power, and spiritual alignment. She is also the founder of Spiritual Black Girl™, a global movement committed to the liberation and elevation of Black women through spiritual restoration, community care, and radical self-love.

Akili believes healing is a birthright, and education is one of its most powerful vehicles. Her mission is to ensure that ancient African wisdom becomes a living, breathing path to liberation for those ready to remember.

# Invitation to Practitioner Training

Become a Certified Kemetic Code™ Practitioner

If this book activated something within you…

If you feel called to not only heal yourself, but to guide others back to their power…

Then your next step may be becoming a certified Kemetic Code™ Practitioner.

At [KemeticCode.com](KemeticCode.com), you'll learn how to:

- Confidently use Sekhem energy and muscle testing to identify and release Knots
- Support individual and collective healing with ancestral wisdom
- Facilitate deep transformation—without burnout or spiritual bypassing

- Build a spiritually aligned practice rooted in Ma'at

Whether you're new to energy work or already hold space as a coach, healer, therapist, or teacher—this path is open to you. The only requirement is your readiness to remember.

Begin your certification journey at <u>KemeticCode.com</u>

## CONTINUE YOUR PERSONAL JOURNEY

If you're not quite ready to become a practitioner but want to go deeper into your own healing and spiritual alignment, join us inside Spiritual Black Girl™.

At <u>SpiritualBlackGirl.com</u>, you'll find:

- Sacred Circles: Monthly virtual gatherings rooted in Ma'at and Kemetic wisdom
- A supportive spiritual community of Black women walking the path with you
- Card decks, eBooks, and guides to deepen your study of Ancient African history and healing practices
- Ongoing tools to help you remember who you are and embody your divine assignment

This is your invitation to reconnect with your roots and rise into your power.

## JOIN THE MOVEMENT AT <u>SPIRITUALBLACKGIRL.COM</u>

# ACKNOWLEDGMENTS

To my husband, Adam – Thank you for walking this journey with me. Your quiet strength and unwavering love have held me through the most transformative seasons. You have given me the space to become who I am, and I'm endlessly grateful.

To my father, Arthur – You opened the door to the wisdom that changed my life. Your teachings sparked the fire in me to study, to question, to remember. You are the root of so much of what I now know to be true.

To my children, Adam and Asia – You are my why. Watching you become who you are reminds me that legacy is not what we leave behind—it's what we live and model right now. Thank you for being my greatest teachers.

To my brother, Jamal – Thank you for reminding me that my voice is my power. You always reflect the truth back to me with love and clarity. As long as I hold on to my voice and my words, I know I will always be good.

*To Adrian, my mentor – Your guidance, protection, and presence have made such a difference in this work. Thank you for seeing me and standing beside me as I brought this vision to life.*

Made in the USA
Columbia, SC
29 May 2025

58213259R10078